the Bridge

Unexpected Help from Life's Crossings

The Bridge

Printed in the United States of America

All scripture refrences are from the King james Version of the Bible, unless otherwise noted.

Ambassador Emerald International
427 Wade Hampton Boulevard
Greenville, S.C. 29609 U.S.A.

and

Ambassador Productions Ltd.
Providence House
Ardenlee Street
Belfast BT6 8QJ, Northern Ireland

www.emeraldhouse.com

Cover design and page layout by A & E Media, Sam Laterza

ISBN 1 889893 92 7

the Bridge

Unexpected Help With Life's Crossings

Betty Rich Hendon with Judy Chatham

DEDICATION

This book is dedicated to the Lamb of God who inspired me to write and who takes away the sins of the world. May it bless the reader and bring glory to the Lord Jesus Christ.

ACKNOWLEDGEMENTS

The journey for this book began twenty years ago. My husband was the first person to give me a push, and Jan Weber was the second. Another teacher and friend, Martha Newsom, volunteered to type my handwritten notes. Billie Cash suggested that I contact Judy Chatham, a writer who worked with me on the manuscript. Both gave me the inspiration that I needed along the way and introduced me to Tomm Knutson, my publisher. Thank you for your faith in this book.

My constant prayer partners included my sister, Verlene Stanfield, and my Bible study group: Becky Sibley, Nell Hawkins, Bonnie Jones, Evie Grimm, Ginger Waugh, Melba Cole, and Paula Alberson. I also want to thank the prayer warriors in Savannah, who included Betty Carlock, Mary Gant, Linda Hill, Tina Rich, Linda Estrada, and Roberta Cude, an award-winning author from my hometown and a former high school friend. Thank you for touching the throne of God with your prayers and support: Wally Weber, Terri Spain, Roy and Barbara Kolwyck, Betty Bennett, Sue Littlejohn, Edna Tate, Faye Carpenter, Rachel Ashmore, Mary Welch, Johnnie Hendon, Jackie Ashpole, and Billie Jean Graham.. Prayers and faith propelled me to bring the book to fruition—a labor of love.

TABLE OF CONTENTS

PROLOGUE

Day after day eagle-eyed, eleven-year-old Betty Joyce stands by her second-story window in the Rich building and sees everything that happens in Savannah, Tennessee. From the time vehicles on U.S. 64 cross the Milo-Lemert Bridge to the time their occupants leave their cars to obtain a court document, to check in at the Farris Hotel; to make a purchase at the Rexall, or to step up to buy a ticket for a movie at Savannah Theater on Courthouse Square—they are being watched.

Young sentinel Betty knows the history well:

"Steamboat's a comin'"

—This announcement brought Savannah, Tennessee, to life in the 1850s. Likewise, in the 1860s the gunfire at nearby Shiloh Church rocked the area and threatened to destroy every town in Hardin County, including lovely Savannah. While its riverfront Cherry Mansion served as headquarters for General Ulysses S. Grant, the armies devoured each other nearby.

Fast forward to the 1940s, the Civil War in the history books, "steamboat's a comin'" dwindled to a faint cry, but one fact survived—the Tennessee River which flows north along beside Savannah continues to excite and even more—give this picture-postcard 7,000 populated town its reason for being.

General Ulysses S. Grant would have agreed with Savannah's fathers when he chose the Tennessee as his thoroughfare to the South. No doubt, Alex and Queen Haley, grandparents of the award-winning *Roots* author, Alex Haley, also saw the Tennessee River and its Savannah landing as the place for them to settle and run a ferry after being freed from slavery.

This river carries with it a rich tradition. Hemmed in by the Mississippi to the West and the Cumberland to the north, the Tennessee drains the middle part of the state by the same name, simultaneously adding great wealth to its river bottom farmland and transporting its goods to points all over the country. However, people like Betty Joyce and the locals revere the Tennessee River, fish, swim, and take in the afternoon sun beside lesser known branches of this great river, such as Turkey Creek, Horse Creek, Indian Creek, and the TVA-inspired Pickwick Reservoir.

The river crawls along the enormous roots, snags and sawyers of trees and underbrush, sometimes even taking a shortcut at one of its bends. The whirlpools and rapids of the Tennessee move the water along until it comes to the landings at Savannah and points beyond.

Many times while following the flow of the Tennessee River, Betty Joyce is joined at the double-wide windows over Courthouse Circle by her Grandfather Oscar Solomon. During those times Papa Os shares the story that explains how Savannah came to be Betty's home. She never tires of hearing him paint the picture of his leaving Alabama to settle in Tennessee. As Papa Os tells his story, Betty tries to comprehend the intensity of his emotions and dreams. Hoping her mind will become steeped with the family's stories she can pass on, Papa Solomon invests heavily into her memory bank. In Betty's writing of this account, Os' granddaughter is fulfilling his highest hopes.

THE BRIDGE FROM OSCAR SOLOMON TO BETTY JOYCE:

Passing the torch…

II Kings 2:13-14 NIV

He picked up the cloak that had fallen from Elijah and went back and stood on the bank of the Jordan. Then he took the cloak that had fallen from him and struck the water, it divided to the right and to the left, and he crossed over.

Fording the Stream

When A Bridge Has Been Provided

Chapter 1

Young Oscar Solomon Establishes The Family Legacy

Around Savannah, Tennessee, exist many bridges—the Harrison-McGarrity, named for Medal of Honor winners from Hardin County, the bridge over Horse Creek, the lower bridge over Indian Creek, the bridge at Burnt Church over Turkey Creek—and there are more. As a product of a river valley, Betty's life has been filled with images of bridges over water, troubled and otherwise. The following story taught her to stop looking for a shallow place to ford, but rather to step up onto the bridge, which is Jesus Christ, the bridge that has already been provided for her.

Oscar Solomon, Betty's maternal grandfather, was a young man determined to succeed at whatever he undertook. As he hitch-hiked from his home in Alabama, thirteen-year-old Os must have rehearsed what he needed to make a way for himself. His lack of reading and writing skills did not stand in his way.

When he was thirteen years old, his mother died, was buried, and, almost immediately, his father remarried. When he and brother Bob announced to Dad that they were going to walk to Savannah, Tennessee, their father was pleased. Times were hard, and he had five children to feed. With the boys on their own, he could provide for the three little girls. Despite the logic, no doubt his father's reaction to their leaving grated on Os' mind as he hiked cross country. One thing he did know—his stepmother had no use for him or his brother and sisters. Also, Os knew that his lack of book-learning and his lack of finances left him with few resources.

In the weeks after he settled in Savannah, Os took on work with area farmers working their land. No sooner had he begun to make his way, did he hear reports that his little sisters were being abused at home. His fiery temperament in his early years may have been born as he began to plot, making plans to deliver his sisters from their abusive home. Os learned the family had left Alabama to find work in Mississippi; by checking with relatives, he knew the location of his father's new farmland. Soon he was on his way to rescue his sisters away.

The course was charted. Fourteen-year-old Os would alternate riding and walking as he and brother Bob approached their father's farmhouse. On the way home Os would stay behind on the horse as the rearguard, and Bob and the girls would walk ahead to safety. No matter--his sisters, Tinnie, Ella and Fannie would soon be safely in the care of Tennessee relatives who had agreed to rear them, for tales of these abuses had reached the Tennessee relatives. No child should have to endure the hardships these children had suffered.

Implementing the plan, Oscar and Bob gathered their three sisters and within days the Solomon family line was securely transferred into Savannah, Tennessee via Cherokee, Alabama.

In the years ahead, Oscar Solomon, a man of focused plans and purposes, first worked on other farmers' land, saved every dime he earned and soon owned his own farmland. Once he had the money to make the purchase, he also wanted a wife. From the moment he set eyes on Clara Gray, he vowed she would someday be his wife. He said, "She's the finest, most beautiful woman in Hardin County. She's a true Southern belle. I will marry her."

And he did.

By 1912 when Os was age 35, he was deemed to be one of the most successful men in Hardin County, Tennessee. On his farmland, he worked from sunup to sundown and became very well versed in the art of horse trading and building a herd of cattle. His philosophy: "Never let the other guy know you want to trade, and if you do trade, make him think trading was his idea."

Questions to Consider:

1. Do you use your gifts and courage for God's glory?

2. If not, how could you reorder your life to do so?

CHAPTER 2

Papa Solomon's Best-laid Plans Turn To Trials

In those days Os was quite a striking figure with his red hair, 6′ frame, and air of confidence. He had a dream and he pursued it. Everyone around admired that. People trusted him, for his word was his bond. After all, he could not write, so he had no use for written contracts. If he signed a contract, he signed it with an X. Though he was frugal with his money, on occasion, he compassionately loaned money on a handshake, but many of these loans were never repaid. Os was a paradigm of complexity with his hot temper and compassionate heart.

The showplace farmhouse he bought for Clara was a two-story white wooden house with arched shuttered windows and guttering that channeled the "rain water" to rain barrels. The front door was set in a triple arch with glass on both sides. Tall white pillars held the roof of the front porch, and all of the woodwork on the front of the house was ornately decorated with cut wood and "gingerbread" design on the railings. Facing south, this lovely home overlooked the pastures and river bottomland where watermelons ripened in the summer sun.

By the time Os was age 29 he and Clara added children to their family. First came Blanche in 1906; then Zelma in 1908; followed by Mabel Elease in 1913. Blanche was fair, had blue eyes and was a true strawberry blonde. Taking on only one part of her father's personality, Blanche was compassionate and kind, coming to know Jesus Christ early in her life. Sweetly, she would curl up in front of the fireplace in the evenings and read from the Bible to her father.

Zelma, at birth, weighed only three pounds. Consequently, her tiny body had to be carried around on a pillow. Then Elease came into the world with perfect health and features, truly a beautiful child upon whom her mother Clara would dote. Clara liked to dress her in beautiful and expensive children's clothing.

Elease, high-spirited and full of fun, enjoyed the parental attention.

All in all, one by one, Oscar's dreams and goals were fulfilled. What a perfect beginning he had enjoyed. He was greatly admired in Hardin County, Tennessee, but all of his hard work was not going to be enough to sustain him. In 1915 when he was 38 years old, his life began to spin out of his control and in a larger sense never did right itself again.

For instance, one Saturday morning, Os realized the insurance on his lovely home had come due. He had planned to ride into Savannah to pay the payment due on that date, but the farm work called to him. Tasks hindered him from riding into town. He reasoned to himself, "I'll just wait until Monday and go by the office and make the payment. Nothing is going to happen in two days."

He was wrong.

During the night that Sunday, Os and Clara smelled smoke. By the time they awakened the children, flames were blazing around the chimney. Reality hit hard. The house was on fire. The children ran to safety, while Os attempted to draw water from the well to pour on the blaze. Clara ran through the house trying to save their clothes and an expensive vase that she valued highly.

"My vase, my vase," she screamed as she threw it out the living room window. Striking the ground, the delicate vase crashed and broke into pieces. That crash, no doubt, was a scene that Clara would replay in her mind over and over again. Its fragile beauty came to an end and seemed to foreshadow the end of what had been an idyllic life as mistress of a large estate.

On this day, Os, rugged and able, could not draw the water fast enough to extinguish the blaze around the chimney, and in the next minutes the house burned to the ground.

One to plan and to focus his efforts, Os was undoubtedly bewildered at this sudden loss. His picture-perfect life had become altered, and he had no means to right it. This burning of his showplace house was not in his control.

However, resilient to the end, Os made immediate plans to rebuild his house on the same site. Since he couldn't receive the insurance money, he had to cut out the details of the house that had made it extraordinary. The ornate extras were not included in the plans, nor did he arch the windows and doors. The guttering had to be omitted too. But soon the family was back in their home again.

The children adjusted to change much more quickly than their parents. The two older girls loved to ride horses over the farmland and often they would put Elease between them and take her riding too.

Then phase two of the shattered dream began to develop. This would be the strike that came like a bolt of lightning from which Os could not recover. His dear sweet Blanche suddenly became ill. The first signs of her illness appeared as leg sores that would not heal. Then she became extremely tired, too exhausted to go to school. "Please let me stay home today; I just don't feel well."

By horse and buggy, desperate Os took his Blanche into Savannah to the doctor's office. Maybe this doctor could cure her illness. But he could not. Determined to see his daughter well again, Os lost no time. Doing the unthinkable in a community where travel by horse and buggy was the norm, he hired a man who owned a car to transport him and his Blanche to Nashville, Tennessee, 138 miles away. A specialist would know how to make her well again.

Meanwhile at home, Blanche's sister and constant playmate, now age 12, had a dream in which Blanche died. In only a month, Blanche, age 14, became morbidly ill, and died in her bed that had been moved beside the fireplace in the dining room. It had been only two months after the specialist at Nashville had examined her and could not make a positive diagnosis.

To say that Oscar Solomon's grief was intense is an understatement, for from the day of Blanche's death when he was 43- years old, he mourned every day until his own death decades later. God worked on his heartstrings and began a process of refining Os, removing some of his fiery temperament and molding him into the man He wanted him to be.

Everyone reacts differently to tragedy. Clara was no exception. In her young years, she, a bit of an opportunist, had married the most-likely-to-succeed man of the area. The "gingerbread" designs in their lives had been stripped when the country home had burned five years before. Os had rebuilt the house and had invited Clara's sister Farra and her aunt Dona to come and live with them to cook, clean and help with the children.

The loss of the trophy house had been a blow to both of them, but buildings could be replaced. Yet nothing in this world could compare with losing his little Blanche. He could not take it all in as he recalled stealing away his little sisters, saving them from harsh treatment, being able to rescue, to save--and then his own daughter had died. He should have been able to save her too.

One either gives in to tragedy or faces it. How would Os react? Clara?

Meanwhile, Clara dealt with her own loss. Life was not working out the way she had planned. Os, no doubt, could see the sadness in her eyes, but his grief was too great to notice all of the signs of her restless spirit.

Nonetheless, twins were soon born to Os and Clara. In an effort to reinvent their lives and try to get beyond their grief, they added Oscar Claude and Clara Maude to the family.

At the same time, the Solomon children lived with their own grief at the loss of their big sister.

As their parents wrestled with the "why?" and "what ifs," the children grew strong in their beliefs that they were sent into the world to right its wrongs. All of them could be as ferocious as Greek warriors, yet on the other hand; they had the compassionate heart of Oscar to match their zeal.

In the ten years that followed the passing of Blanche, Os developed a most debilitating form of rheumatoid arthritis. Probably this illness was a result of a genetic pre-disposition, but one has to wonder if grief had something to do with the severity of his condition. Working from sun-up to sun-down in the icy cold had an effect on his fingers, knees, and toes until he began to live and work with pain as his companion. By age 53, Os, the respected farmer, horse trader and owner of a large herd of cattle, was unable to do the work on his land. His only son, Claude, was a preschooler and would be unable to assist for a number of years.

In an effort to regain his health, Os checked in at Warm Springs, Georgia, and Hot Springs, Arkansas, to receive treatment for the arthritis. All help was temporary. The doctors would tell him he had to stop working, but he would not stop. He needed to continue to work, for he was too young to retire. The determination to succeed continued to live somewhere under the layers of grief. The year was now 1930.

In the Depression Years everything around Oscar was changing fast, and unknown to him he would add to the string of great disappointments: the loss of the lavish home, the death of his child, and the debilitating arthritis.

First, Clara suggested they buy a business on Main Street in Savannah where she ran a store selling men's and women's clothing, domestic goods and lace. Os, now unable to handle his horse and buggy, bought himself a Model T Ford. In the ten years since the death of Blanche, his 6-foot frame had become so debilitated he could no longer bend over nor could he close his hands in a grip. He weighed only 150 lbs. He had to own a car to transport himself into town.

Driving his new car down the lane to his farmhouse, he headed for the shed built onto his smokehouse. He didn't put on the brakes and flew through the back wall of the shed into the family plot where his relatives were buried, through the barnyard, scattering chickens in all directions. The car continued on in a circular motion until it coughed and sputtered to a stop. It had run out of gas. For weeks, Os' first night in his Model T became the talk of the neighborhood.

Clara, meanwhile, was greatly enjoying her time at the store. She had been cloistered out on the farm for years and now she could pursue the conversations and life of a lady who knew what was going on in the area. Perhaps feeling left behind, Os soon rented the farm to another farmer and moved within eight blocks of town. All of these developments were totally against his way of doing things, but he was seeing that Clara was going on with her life, and he had become a person bound to his chair.

All of his efforts to keep Clara satisfied failed in that year of 1930 when, finally, Clara filed for divorce. She took the house in town for a short time, then moved to Memphis and on to Miami, Florida, near her brother stationed in the U.S. Army. The twins remained in Savannah with their father until years later when they lived for periods of time with their mother.

The decades passed. The arthritis in Os' body destroyed his joints; yet, he lived on in great pain every minute of every day.

Meanwhile, life was better for Clara. She soon began working for a realtor and became a success at buying and selling houses. Her family rarely knew her address because she would buy a house, move in, and then sell it. Always she made money on the deal. Many of her letters began "My new address is."

The more immobilized Os became, the more animated Clara became. She came into the homes of her relatives and immediately had ideas for rearranging furniture and making changes that complimented the style of the moment. She dressed flamboyantly and succeeded in the world of real estate as Miami's population increased. Life was a whirl of enjoyment to her, for she was never bored. Perhaps she was remembering those somber, grief-stricken days on the farm and never wanted to revisit those days again. Perhaps she was burying them behind a curtain of activity.

Debilitated for nearly twenty years, Os came to his daughter Zelma's house in Savannah and sat on the stool near the window of their upstairs apartment that overlooked courthouse circle. And there he told the stories of his life to his granddaughter, Betty Joyce.

Then at age 80, Oscar Solomon, horse trader, successful landowner, loving husband and doting father, endured yet another blow to his life. Both legs were amputated just above the knees. The poor circulation in his legs had taken its toll and gangrene now threatened his life.

The day of the amputation came and went. His mind remained sharp. He recovered somewhat, but only a few years later he had to enter the Hardin County Nursing Home in Patterson Woods. From the day he entered this facility until his death he had to have two aspirin every four hours for pain. Some family members believed that this was a factor in his alertness and longevity. He died at age 93 in 1970.

Earlier, Clara had married John Holloway, and the two lived in Miami until John retired. The couple moved to Savannah, and John and Os became good friends.

Ironically, Clara died one year before Os died. Over the years Zelma had cautioned her father "Do not be bitter that Mom left you."

He always said, "I won't be."

Oscar Solomon, good looking, hardworking, redheaded, strong, passionate, able, was one colorful man of his time. He never knew for certain his exact birth date, nor did he ever learn to read or write; yet he persevered, and he, with God's help, dealt with all of the obstacles of his life.

Questions to Consider:

1. Do you see a ceiling on what an individual could accomplish without God in his plans?

2. Could it be that God allows us to succeed over and over again, and then allows us to run in circles and sputter until we run out of gas---all in hope we will run to Him?

3. To what are you devoting most of your energy each day?

Chapter 3

From Patterson Place to Bad Alley

From Papa Os' story, Betty started to draw her own conclusions. She was only eleven years old, but she was old enough to see where Papa Os had made some mistakes along the way.

Here is her story:

When I was nine years old, my family moved into a house with an inviting history. I am certain that when we moved into this fading Southern mansion, my father, Clyde Rich, thought we were ascending the ladder of success. Little did he know the influence our one year of living in the revered Patterson Place would have on my life.

I remember the document that sealed the deal:

> I, Mildred Patterson, one of the children and lawful heirs of A.M. Patterson, deceased, acting as an agent for the other heirs, have this day leased unto Clyde Rich of Savannah, Tennessee, the A.M. Patterson residence, together with the barn, cow pasture at the rate of forty dollars per month, the first payment due October 1, 1945.

As an addendum:

> There is a library room upstairs that is used only for shelves of books, and the said Clyde Rich, will be permitted use of said room.

A. M. Patterson, a prominent lawyer and landowner, left an interesting legacy in the Savannah area. As in any life not everything turned out as he had planned, but for the most part, he led an industrious life and added much to his community. His first marriage, which produced daughter Dorothy, had ended tragically as the ship his young wife took out of Savannah sank. Then

Arch remarried and into this union came Mildred, Marie, DeWitt, Edmund, Betsy and Grace. These children and their parents were the first occupants of the lovely Patterson Place mansion.

In the years I had lived across the street from Patterson Place, I assumed this place was built for someone very special. Even after the death of A.M. Patterson, it never occurred to me that our family would soon move in. Happy and yet reluctant to move, I said goodbye to my playhouse and to my rooster Tom. We took the cow and moved across the road to indoor plumbing and leather bound books in the upstairs library. Moving day came and went as members of the Rich family settled into their daily routine of school for two children, work for H.C.and Dad, and cooking and housekeeping for Mother.

From day one, we children explored the Patterson Place. With wide eyes, I endeavored to take it all in. Soon the front porch swing and the second story library became my favorites. My best friend, Becky Ross, and I enjoyed the motion of swinging in that large, white wooden swing. The open library flowed into a large area at the top of the stairs with five bedrooms and a sun porch surrounding and opening into these book-lined walls. While only the library had been leased to us, we continued to explore. Soon we could see how the Pattersons had occupied this palatial home. As I sat cross-legged in the middle of the library reading my favorite, a book a poetry, I could only guess what was behind the locked bedroom doors leading off from the library.

In the tradition of all Southern mansions, a grand hallway divided the lower floor of the house. I noted that this hallway was four times the width of the hallway in our old house. Upon opening the front door, I could see the parlor with the two baby grand pianos, one with the usual curving lines and the other an unusual square. A hall closet now contained my school clothes that Mother had ordered from Sears and Roebuck catalogue. One yellow dress was especially worthy of its new surroundings. It had small flowers all over the skirt with small pinched pleats on the bodice.

Across the hall from the parlor was the dining room. For someone older, this dining room might have looked faded and out of date, but for me, the room came to life. All along the top of the wainscot paneling were the faded impressions of the Patterson fine bone china plates. Even though the plates had been removed, these circles gave the room a majestic aura.

My young eyes were impressed with the wealth that I could surmise from the sizes of the rooms and what the family had left behind. Did these surviving Patterson heirs have so much wealth they could afford to leave behind their leather-bound books and their two baby grand pianos?

The real plus to living at Patterson Place was the proximity to a celebrity, Mary Elizabeth Patterson, the actress who was their relative. Elizabeth, born on November 22, 1874, had starred in "Tobacco Road," "Belle Star," "Intruder in the Dust," and "So Red the Rose." In fact, during the 1930s she had starred in 33 films (The Courier). As one could guess, the Pattersons initially did not want their lovely daughter Elizabeth to become an actress. In fact, her grandparents didn't either, but they sent her the money to go to acting school. In later years she rewarded them. When she came home to Savannah, she brought glamour and excitement. The story goes that on one of these occasions, she was riding down Main Street and happened to notice that the Methodist Church had a makeshift steeple on its roof. The wind had damaged the earlier steeple, and the parishioners had decided to erect one quickly using whatever materials they had on hand. Elizabeth, thinking this new steeple was a travesty, announced that she wanted that chicken coop taken down at once. She then gave the money for a new steeple to be erected and also gave money for some new chairs for the church choir. She always came to town with many hatboxes, furs and many, many suitcases. Always she brought gifts for the whole family. Most people in Savannah felt close enough to her to call her Aunt Mary.

Very soon after I had begun to follow the career of Elizabeth Patterson, I learned she had taken the role of Ms. Trumble, the elderly babysitter to Lucy and Desi's children on the "I Love Lucy" show. With television coming into its own, being on one of the most loved television shows was success personified.

An acquaintance of my father came by our house a few years after we had moved away from this landmark and talked to Dad about the Pattersons. As always, I listened.

I learned that the youngest daughter Grace, now age 21, had gone to live with relatives after her father, A. M. had died seven years earlier. She attended high school in various locations before graduating. Then she went on to attend various colleges—first Washington University in St. Louis, then George Peabody in Nashville, next Randolph-Macon Women's College in Lynchburg, Virginia. Following a very serious car accident, she had finished her undergraduate work with honors in economics at the University of Arizona. Many in Savannah had talked about the difficulty uprooted Grace had endured after her father's passing, but a member of the family painted a picture of their idyllic early days while living at Patterson Place (The Courier).

A.M. Patterson, the youngest of seven children and a prominent lawyer in Savannah, married Marie Elizabeth, a lovely school teacher, who arrived one sunny day aboard a steamboat. In the following years, Marie was an active mother of six children. She founded the PTA in Savannah schools, was active in the DAR, the United Daughters of the Confederacy, and was the first woman school board member of this small town. Sadly, this larger than life woman died when Grace was only seven years old (The Courier).

In the years that followed, Grace told friends in Savannah that her father A.M. was a strict disciplinarian, but also had a gentle spirit. "He loved to sing, and when he was a student at Vanderbilt, he sang in the famous Glee Club which made a world tour." Grace had been asked to join the Sub Deb Club, a social club for the elite in Savannah's society scene. She declared she had no idea why she had been invited, "I never really fit in. My father wouldn't let me go to town in the afternoons when school was out, like the rest of the crowd did. He told me that if I had some business to attend to, I could go but otherwise I was to go home."(The Courier).

Then, seven years after her mother died when Grace was age 14, Grace's father A.M. Patterson, who was the great stabilizing force in her life, died. Not only had she lost her parents, but her secure and prominent life at Patterson Place came to an end. It was said that A.M. left Grace plenty of money to complete her high school and college expenses. Nonetheless, her life at Patterson Place in Savannah had ended (The Courier).

Adding up the years and discovering that stately, cypress-shingled Patterson Place had been closed three years when our little family moved into the public rooms, I moved on. I could identify with Grace's dilemma over wanting to go downtown like the other kids did. My own father had forbid me to go to certain sections of the town. One street, Bad Alley, was not far from Courthouse Circle. (Today it is Guinn and Court, but then it was known as Bad Alley.)

Bad Alley earned its reputation for its brawls, fowl language, fights, and by the murders that occurred in this part of Savannah from time to time. In the early 1940s it was no place for a lady or children. At that time it was the place where tempers flared and bullets flew. Sheriff Fred Stricklin was the keeper of law and order until he lost his life to one of these Bad Alley bullets. Dutifully, I stayed clear of this area until new businesses went in replacing the rough cafes that once ran a thriving business.

Questions to Consider:

1. Is it possible that you could live in a place with such rich history, industry and beauty that its loveliness seems to be all that you need?
2. At what point do people usually discover that in this life, even with its natural beauty, all of us need a Savior?
3. What choices are you making regarding where you will go with your own life?

Deuteronomy 29 and 30

Moses' last words serve as a bridge to the future.

CHOOSE LIFE.
Choose God's way and you choose life; serve idols and choose certain death.

*The Courier, Savannah, Tennessee, Summer Visitor's Guide, 1998.

CHAPTER 4

ONE FIGHTS FOR THE UNION, ANOTHER FOR THE CONFEDERACY

Daily I looked out the window and saw Raymond's taxi parked in the first parking space on Court Square by the side of Stephen's market, and I heard the phone inside Elbert Williams' Barber Shop across the street. Since there was no air conditioning, all of our windows were raised and the ringing was too loud to overlook.

Mr. Shelby usually sat in his taxi waiting for a call, and I watched him open the door of his car and walk to the Williams Barber Shop to answer his phone.

In Savannah we had an abundance of taxis. Mangum's, Cromwell's, and McKnight's taxis parked on Guinn Street whereas Jerrold's cab usually parked on Court Square. My Grandmother Oma was a sister to Roberta's mother, Aunt Mollie Neill. Aunt Mollie received visions from God, and I was impressed to know someone that close to God. Likewise, I was impressed with Aunt Mollie's husband's unusual name--Greenhaw Smith.

One day in the 1940s, Buster, the barber in the first chair at Williams Barber Shop, had a bird's eye view of one of Savannah's notorious killings—the murder of a local man by a deputy. The man had just paid the barber for a haircut and had walked outside on the sidewalk when he met the deputy and asked him to stop setting a bad example for his kids. He was referring to the well-known reported gossip that the deputy was seeing his pretty married neighbor. The angry deputy pulled his gun and killed the man on the spot.

From my perch in the window above Main Street, I was sure the second barber Punkin' had witnessed the bloody scene that day. Scared, shaking, I could not ignore what I heard below with all of the loud talking and even louder gunshot. Safe in my apartment above the fray below, I saw a crowd rush to the scene of the tragedy, but that night I accompanied Mom and Dad to pay their respects to the widow. The deceased had been a good friend of my parents.

While there was rarely an uneventful moment on Savannah's Courthouse Square, I sometimes felt it was a wonderful respite to leave the window ledge and go over to Fairground Street to visit my grandmother Oma.

When I did, I often went into her bedroom, and there were the pictures of my two ancestors looking down on the beds. While there were many interesting places to play in Grandmother Oma's flower gardens or under her trellises, one attraction caused me to pester my Grandmother with many questions—the pictures of the two daring soldiers facing Oma and Poney's beds in the master bedroom. Alfred Alexander Neill, the Confederate, hung facing his daughter Oma's bed. William Franklin Rich, Union soldier in the 10th Infantry Tennessee Regiment, hung facing his son Poney's bed. No doubt in the days of their battlefield fighting neither of these soldiers envisioned a day when their pictures would hang side by side or even worse that, their children would unite. Unknowingly as they had fought in the bloody Civil War battles, they had built a bridge—the bridge that had produced our family.

I entertained myself with stories of the past, regarding the period when the Union Army had come into Savannah in March of 1862. Vicki Betts of the local Hardin County Society (The Hardin County Historian Quarterly) had written an account. The story goes that as early as Feb 6, 1862, the citizens were forewarned that their area might be the site of one of the Civil War battles. A passenger from one of the steamboats that traveled their way jumped overboard, swam to shore and announced that Yankee gunboats would surely be heading this way. By March 1, the "Tyler" and the "Lexington" came to patrol the river.

I enjoyed reading about the events that surrounded my hometown, and I was fascinated by my mother's story about the little drummer boy. Miss Betts in the Hardin County Historical Society told that story, "In the face of imminent invasion, on Thursday March 6, Confederate officials at Savannah held their part of a statewide enrollment of men of military age. Word of the draft soon traveled down river. Immediately, about half of the 40th Illinois Infantry came to occupy Savannah. Soon making themselves at home, they sent out patrols and pickets to check out enemy fire in the area."

During Saturday night, March 8 around a thousand drafted Union soldiers came from both sides of the river to join about 500 recruits from around the area. Some local citizens, fearing Confederate retaliation, asked to relocate their families.

On Sunday afternoon, March 9, the "Lexington" gunboat traveled upstream and lobbed about a dozen shells into nearby Pittsburg Landing. No responsecame fromthe Confederates.

By Monday, March 10, Union soldiers were becoming ill. William Cherry, the town's leading Unionist, a wealthy planter, merchant, and Hardin County's fifth largest slave holder, opened a local home as a hospital. Town officials also volunteered a new frame church so that local citizens could make the soldiers more comfortable.

It was March 11, Tuesday that the people of Savannah would never forget. Miss Betts' account states,

"About noon the steamer "Golden Gate" arrived, announcing that the main body of the western federal army was just behind it. The 46th Ohio and probably everyone else in Savannah, gathered on the hill above the landing, peering down the river as far as they could see. By two o'clock the lead boat came into sight."

One witness of this event wrote: "The weather was soft and fine, and one or more flags floated over every boat. Nearly every regiment had a band of music, and in this, until then, sequestered region, occurred a scene of martial activity and festivity, never before witnessed in the Union. Unexpected, grand, and, indeed terrible, it was, to the inhabitants along the forest-girded banks of the Tennessee."

Betts continues, "The fleet included up to a hundred steamers laden to the guards with soldiers, cattle, and munitions of war. The decks were dark with blue-coated soldiers. Bright brass cannon glittered on the foredeck, where the batteries were loaded, and the band played their most soul-stirring airs. The transports sent forth vast volumes of smoke, which shadowed and besotted the atmosphere from hill to hill across the river valley. They docked at Savannah, on both sides of the river for a mile, at places four or five deep. At night the bright lights on either shore looked like 'so many will-o-the-wisps dancing over the water.'"

The charm of the arriving Union army soon gave way to unsanitary conditions, malaria, dysentery, and typhoid fever. Savannah turned into one huge hospital.

On March 16 General William T. Sherman had located his troops upstream at Pittsburg Landing. The following day, General U.S. Grant arrived at Savannah and Sherman urged that the army be moved to that more strategic location, Pittsburg Landing. Grant ordered all of the troops still on the gunboats to Pittsburg Landing, leaving only one division encamped around Savannah.

Oddly, on April 6, one of the most important battles of the Civil War would soon be fought on thist quiet lovely area along the Tennessee River. Inland from Pittsburg Landing, were a few scattered landowners growing mostly corn, cotton, and sweet potatoes. Only 23 slaves lived in the whole district. The fields were merely clearings in the forest, and the few houses were log cabins.

Shiloh Church, a Methodist meeting house, was described as a one-room log cabin, originally chinked, with a clapboard roof and plain benches—a building that would "make a good corncrib for an Illinois farmer." From scouting reports most of the residents of this quiet area had left their homes at the early sight of the approaching armies. At one homestead only the family's rooster had been left behind.

Some of the people of nearby Savannah served as guides for the Union soldiers, but also provided much needed information to the Confederate soldiers, for families of Savannah were split in their loyalties during the Civil War.

I recall a humorous story my grandmother Oma and other relatives told about her father Alfred Alexander Neill, a Confederate, coming home after the latest skirmish of the war. Coming down the rutted lane, he saw up ahead that his own farm near Neill Cemetery had been taken over by a group of Yankee soldiers.

Surely this occupation of his land was the ultimate insult to the war-weary soldier coming home to his family. Having worn no Confederate uniform home, he walked on and soon joined the happy crowd of Union soldiers who were clustered around his well. They drew a bucket of water, and thinking he was merely one of the locals, offered him a drink from their water bucket. Then he proceeded to compare war notes with them, conversing as though he were joining old friends. When he had learned many important details concerning the Union Army's supplies, horses and future plans, he went inside the house and joined his family for the night.

Then, along about 3:00 a.m., when he felt certain the Yankees were sleeping soundly, he slipped outside and, knowing the grade of his property well, hardly stumbled in the dark as he untied the horses of his unwanted guests. Hurriedly he mounted one and ushered the others ahead of him to be used by the Confederate army in the next battle against these Union occupants of his farm.

All of these tales and historical events were the backdrop for shaping my early formative years when I came on the scene in 1935—to a family of avid storytellers.

Such were the stories of the occupation of both Union and Confederate soldiers in and around Savannah during the Civil War. While I hardly enjoyed the idea of a war between those who had been comrades, I did think my hometown a special place to live with all of the sideline stories of the well-known Battle of Shiloh. Plus I felt I owed it to take note for these soldiers whose pictures looked down upon my grandparent's beds.

One of the residents of the area, Inez Franks Cooper, had told a story of her grandmother's seeing the Union Army marching down the road near her house (Hardin County Historical Society, The Hardin County Historian Quarterly).

It was a warm day in April 1862. Lissie had moved her invalid husband's sick bed to the front porch so he could enjoy some fresh air. What she did not know was that General U.S. Grant and General Sherman had brought thousands of Union troops south by way of the Tennessee River. And these thousands of soldiers were waiting for General Don Carlos Buell to bring the Union army of Ohio to join them.

Lissie also did not know that about 30 miles away at a little church named Shiloh the Confederate Army was quietly gathering and camping in wait for the first fire to start off a major battle.

As Lissie swatted at the flies that hovered over her husband's sickbed, she looked up and saw the vanguard of a huge army advance toward her house. Transfixed, she stood admiring the beautiful blue uniforms, the blaze of color from the flags. How beautiful was this sight! Impulsively she unwound a white cloth and began to wave it back and forth as the marching columns came nearer to her house.

Immediately the command and the whole army came to a halt right in front of her. Mounted officers up front rode briskly to the rear. Lizzie stood frozen in place, for she feared she had offended this great mass of well-armed men. Yet the army in front of her soon resumed marching as if nothing at happened, but she knew she had been noticed.

Led by a mounted officer, the regimental band swung out of the line of march and halted squarely in front of her front porch. Then they played an entire rendition of the most popular tune of the day and turned to leave. She asked for more.

The officer said with a wry grin on his face, "Our orders are to play a tune for each 'salute' we receive from the local populace as we pass through…but only one tune per 'salute.' Yours is the only such 'salute' we have received since leaving Nashville. Good day to you."

They marched on, but a sickly Ohio soldier was left in Lissie's care. He died while there and was buried in the orchard with a plain stone marker.

The Hardin County historian Vicki Betts reported that the Union Army moved on past Savannah about eight miles upstream to Pittsburg Landing. There they drilled, enjoyed the beginning of a Tennessee spring. General Grant set up his headquarters back in Savannah in the beautiful Cherry Mansion overlooking the Tennessee River where tiny lavender violets carpeted the riverbank.

Today I can see General Grant as he walked the grounds located behind Cherry's Truck Stop. These were the same grounds where I watched the peacocks strut as I ate warm pecan pie baked by Mrs. Frank Cherry's sister. As I ate, I could hear the orders General Grant barked to his men down on the docks. To make it all come to life, I looked at pictures we had in our family photo album. We had pictures of my grandparents, of my mother, and of me beside the Cherry Mansion, Grant's headquarters, in the background. This U.S. Grant command post had been only three blocks from my home.

The story goes that as General Grant paced the grounds of the Cherry Mansion, wives of many of the soldiers arrived by steamer. They had followed their husbands into the area, many thinking they could help by being nearby. As a result of this addition, in early April General Grant wrote to his own wife saying she must stay home for he was going to have to halt the arrival of all of these wives. After all, he assured his wife of his desire to build an efficient army here.

Sunday, April 6 General Grant awoke nursing a badly sprained ankle. In one of the upstairs rooms of the Cherry Mansion, he dressed and went down for breakfast, but had not even tasted his coffee when he was informed of heavy gunfire upriver. His saddled horse was immediately loaded on the already stoked "Tigress," and he left for Shiloh's "dark and bloody ground."

The fighting went on all day, with the federal gunboats shelling at fifteen-minute intervals all night, then the battle continuing into Monday.

Having been surprised by the encamped army of the Confederates at Shiloh Church, many of the Union army swam out to gunboats at Pittsburg Landing to safety. Soon the gunboats became overcrowded as the Union soldiers were hanging on for dear life. Just before they sank, the captain had to step to the side of the boat with a hatchet and yell to them that he would kill them if they did not swim to another gunboat for this one was sinking. Yet more came and clung to the gunboat, and the captain used his hatchet to chop off fingers and hands forcing the remaining swimmers to swim on to other gunboats.

The sound of battle could be heard for miles. The Hardin County Historical Society story goes that Caldonia Banks, on the western edge of neighboring Wayne County twenty-five miles away, was at a spring, drawing water for the day. "She raised up and looked around to see from which direction the loud noise was coming. No cloud was in the sky but the rumbling continued. Later in the day, the rumble changed to 'boom-boom-boom.'" The noise continued on into the next day, and Caldonia had no idea what was causing it.

Likewise, four or five miles beyond Savannah, a Union soldier marching into Savannah with the Sherman Brigade could hear the cannon clearly and distinctly, the volleys of the muskets. On this Monday in Savannah, the Brigade found a "scene of the utmost confusion and excitement." All through the night steamboats had been running between Pittsburg Landing and Savannah, taking in troops and ammunition and returning with wounded men from the day's battle.

The Union soldier continues, "All of the buildings in the little straggling village had been taken possession of for hospital purposes. Here and there, on porches and in yards, lay the bodies of those who had died during the night. In almost every house surgeons were at work dressing wounds and amputating shattered limbs. As we marched down the main street toward the river we could hear on every side the groans of the suffering."

Meanwhile local men had fought on both sides that day, and the people of Savannah wanted to go to the battlefield to search for loved ones as soon as the volleys stopped.

This Battle of Shiloh would later be known as one of the first blood baths of large proportion of the Civil War. And such a close call—both sides with around 10,000 casualties.

I had to wonder what would have happened if General Buell's regiment had been held up by other area people waving white dish cloths. Is it possible that the Civil War would have ended right then?

At home, we had family photographs taken at Shiloh National Military Park--pictures of my parents, Clyde (grandson of William Franklin Rich and Alex Neill) and Zelma in front of the monuments to fallen heroes--pictures in front of stacked cannon balls and cannons. There were pictures where we were enjoying an outing. In one picture, Mother, almost bent over with laughter, stands before a monument.

One has to view such a setting with some degree of detachment. Otherwise, how could the residents of Savannah and Hardin County have enjoyed living in the shadow of this battlefield where 20,000 men had lost their limbs or their lives?

So were my thoughts as great granddaughter of two of the principal soldiers who fought in Civil War battles. Quietly they looked over the bedroom of Oma and Poney, but how fierce they had been as they fought against each other.

As at regular intervals in my childhood I thought about that awful day at Shiloh, I began to see that a person then, nor a person in my day, could continue to ford the streams of life, but rather they must stop fighting, stop sinking the overcrowded boats and start looking for a solution to conflict.

Look for the bridge that has been provided.

Questions to Consider:

1. Even though you may not have relatives who are on opposite sides of a conflict, do you have family members who have feuded for decades?

2. Are you looking for the bridge God has provided for you in your life?

3. How can you help people who wrestle with bridging their anger and differences with other individuals?

Chapter 5

A TENT REVIVAL, LIFE'S MEANING UNFOLDS

As a child watching over the Courthouse Circle, I contemplated what it meant to live in Stringtown, a part of Savannah across a stream and devoted to the African American population of Savannah. I visualized how first one, then another Black man or woman had found their places of employment somewhere along the Tennessee River. Often they worked for large landowners toting their products onto barges headed for New Orleans markets. Some women were domestic help in the large mansions that had been built along the river bluffs. One such man and woman were Alex and Queen Haley, later known nationally as the grandparents of prize-winning author Alex Haley. The elder Alex, whose story Papa Os had told, had settled in Savannah to run the ferry that crossed the Tennessee River at the edge of town. His wife, Queen, had served as domestic help in the Cherry Mansion. Alex' ferry operation had been overtaken when the Milo-Lemert Bridge was dedicated about 1930. Of course, by that time, he was an elderly man and, like the rest of us welcomed the bridge that replaced his ferryboat business.

Dunbar High School girls had a basketball team that was not to be reckoned with. I often wondered if the girls in Stringtown and New Town wondered what it would be like to be a white girl on my side of Savannah, but I just took life as it came by spending most of my time after school playing paper dolls at Betty Jane Thompson's, or pitching washers with Shirley Hudson at Mrs. Arch Walker's house. My eagle eyes took in different family units as I added new friends along the way—Lawanna Walker, Winnie Gale Shutt, Helen Joyce Whitlow, Mary Jene Johnson and Helen Jean Wolfe. As was typically southern, most of us went by double names.

Nonetheless, as I had spent much of my childhood observing it was now time for me to starting thinking about my own values, morals and future. It was when I was eleven years old that I began to look for my bridge in life. My mother did her part in helping me find it. She chose not to rear an undisciplined child—so I was lovingly shaped into a vessel God could use.

Mother had been a housewife until she accepted a position in a button factory. There she worked for one year from 3:00 to 11:00 p.m. and then began helping Daddy at Rich's Market. He had opened the grocery after closing the Firestone Store and leasing parts of our building over the years.

Rich's Market represented a time of transition before Daddy, Clyde "Cubby" Rich, built the restaurant and motel at Pickwick when I was in my adolescent years. That's when my search for my own identity began in earnest.

This restaurant came at the time when I was beginning to notice my place in the peer group. I was at the stage in life that I wanted to be like everyone else, yet wanted to shine just a little more brightly, to be the best student, to dress well, to be popular--all of those things the world around had conditioned me to strive for. Just as the heat of peer pressure hit its mark, I became the daughter of the owner of a new restaurant and motel which catered to fishermen and was located near Pickwick Lake, the preferred hangout of young people in Savannah. What a lucky break for me! I liked to be near water, and the view at the lake was eye-catching.

Pickwick was, and is, also the setting for the annual Catfish Festival in the summertime. "No where do the catfish grow plumper and tastier than at Pickwick." It was here that a girl I had greatly admired became the first Catfish Queen. Mary Frances Cherry, a tall, willowy blonde with perfect features and a winning personality, was to me the prettiest girl in town. She was my role model who lived a block from me and was a year ahead of me in school. Her life looked very glamorous.

Within a few blocks of my house were three churches, the Church of Christ, the Baptist Church, and the Methodist Church. My first prerequisite was that the church had to be within walking distance. My second prerequisite for selecting a church was having a classmate with whom to sit. Since my friends, Cornelia Turman, Karen Alexander, and her sister Shirley, attended the closest church, I chose to walk past the post office and Massey Boaz's ice plant to this church. But very soon when Shirley Hudson invited me to go with her to her church, I readily agreed when I heard that another classmate, Peggy Lowder, attended. How fickle I was at this early age!

Our Sunday school room was in the basement of the church with Peggy's mother as the teacher. On some occasions I ate Sunday dinner with the Lowders, and at other times Peggy ate at our house. We usually played games because Sunday was a day when we could not go to the movies. At this time the belief was that to keep the Sabbath holy one did not go to the movies.

I faithfully did not miss a Sunday for one full year. Then I proudly accepted my perfect attendance pin. After church I always went home to read my favorite cartoons in the Sunday funny paper—"Nancy" by Ernie Bushmiller and "Mutt and Jeff" by Bud Fisher.

Life was good.

When I was eleven years old, a tent revival, a common summer happening in Savannah, a typical "Bible Belt" town, was scheduled. The music was good and emotions ran high. This was a spirited congregation.

Being already familiar with "church things" and the Spirit of the Lord, I took this tent revival meeting message in stride. After all, every Sunday morning I walked to the big church a few blocks from my home. I liked church and was curious to know more. Without realizing it, I was ready for a spiritual awakening.

Even though I had perfect attendance that year in Sunday school, I wasn't a Christian. I had never accepted Jesus as my Savior. But during this revival, I had a personal experience with the Lord. I don't recall the topic of the sermon, but I do remember the strong calling of the Holy Spirit.

When the Holy Spirit spoke to my heart, I thought about going to the front altar and professing my faith in God, but I listened to a voice that reminded me that others might think such a move very strange.

"What will Mary Frances Cherry think of you if you go up front?" this inner voice questioned.

She lived a block from me; in my eyes, her life was perfect.

But the call from God proved more urgent than the call from the adversary. The sweet presence of God seemed so real, and the Holy Spirit continued to tug at my heart. With tears streaming down my face, I went up front to bow at the altar beside Barbara Lackey, Carolyn Deberry, Betty Milam, Becky, and Verlene.

Later I realized that the thought of Mary Frances' acceptance of my decision was merely a trick of the devil—a ploy to hold me in my seat. Besides, as I thought about the matter, I knew she was a faithful member of her own church.

I remember the feeling I felt when I accepted Jesus Christ and what He had done for me on the cross. I'd never felt so clean in all of my life. Surprise and delight surged through me like the sensation of discovering a familiar tree in a forest in which I had been roaming lost. Besides, I had just had my first real conversation with my Father. I seemed sequestered from hurt, from pain, and from evil, and peace reigned.

Yes, I saw Main Street that night with new eyes. As we passed Yeiser's Chevrolet and the Health Department, I remember thinking that I wanted to feel this squeaky clean for the rest of my life. I knew for sure that if I died tonight, I would go straight to heaven. **Psalm 51:7 "Wash me and I shall be whiter than snow**."

God's Holy Spirit had won the battle for my soul on that day, September 12, 1947, one month before I was twelve years old.

Only a few days later on a hot September day in 1947, I was baptized in Horse Creek, along with my sister Verlene, my best friend Becky, and about ten other young people.

Horse Creek was one of the main streams near our town, all of which had some kind of tie to my family. There were Turkey Creek, Indian Creek and others, and then there was Horse Creek, which meandered along Highway 64 behind J. I. Bell's house and farm (now a Wal-Mart store). On the day of my baptism I could not help but remember that only a few years earlier I had run from a mad bull in this same area. It had been on the occasion of my accompanying my Daddy to throw out his baited line to catch catfish. But now as I was coming up out of the waters of Horse Creek, that bull-chasing day was the least of my concerns. Indeed I was "a new creature in Christ."

Now I had the Holy Spirit in my life, and He would teach me new Spiritual things. What a difference those thirty minutes at the altar made in the course of my life. The results of this one decision would influence my choice of college, my choice of profession, my choice of life mate and the area of the country where I would live out the next several decades. This choice had far-reaching influence.

"Where He leads me, I will Follow" became the song in my heart and my grades in school began to reflect this transformation. Suddenly I had higher expectations for myself. All I wanted to do was please God. I remember that I read about

Daniel of the Bible, and I wanted to be like him—making wise decisions and bringing glory to God.

"Now I know the plans I have for you," declares the Lord. **"Plans to prosper you and not to harm you, plans to give you hope and a future." Jeremiah 29:11**

With my new eyes I began to apply my new way of life to the happenings in school and in our local news. Therefore, when one of my classmates who lived in the same house where I had once lived, told of her late night escapades, I was appalled.

She, an eighth grader, told me that when her parents were asleep, she slipped out her window and rushed to get in the car with her boyfriend, a taxicab driver in town. Month after month I watched her life choices.

Many years later, tragedy struck; she was killed one night as she was leaving a night spot along the highway outside of town. This tragic story and many others that I heard my friends discuss affected my life greatly. I felt I could see the consequences of choices that were not in God's will. I hoped that she had accepted Jesus as her Savior before she drew her last breath that final night.

James 3: 17 "But the wisdom that is from above, is first pure, then peaceable, gentle...full of mercy and good fruits."

My sister Verlene and I were united in two ways now—united as sisters and united in the family of God, for she had allowed God to come into her life two nights before I accepted Christ.

At the tent revival meeting I had found Jesus, THE BRIDGE.

Something had changed—I felt ALIVE IN CHRIST, and I had an inner peace.

With all of this awakening, I gravitated toward the occupation I would have in my later life. I loved reading and the study of American and English literature.

My schoolteachers greatly influenced me. My ninth-grade English teacher, Mrs. Sevier, said, "A person is not really educated until she has read the novel *Jane Eyre* by Charlotte Bronte." Of course, the following afternoon, Emma Bolyard had a visitor in the courthouse library. I checked out Jane Eyre and read into late each night. I loved being transplanted to the moors. Then after *Jane Eyre*, I checked out the novel by her sister Emily Bronte, *Wuthering Heights*.

Others in the community influenced me. On my 14th birthday, October 29, 1949, I remember walking upstairs from Main Street to Hitt's Studio, and there Clara Hitt took my picture. Miss Hitt had posed me and said, "You have a pretty complexion, Betty." I remember going home and looking in the mirror at my complexion. I had never thought about my coloring before that day. Her words pleased me. The words that people say do have an effect on our lives.

What I did not know on that day—four years earlier Miss Hitt had taken the picture of another fourteen year old, a young man who would become my husband eight years later. In fact, I had never seen this boy who lived about 200 feet off Highway 64, just six miles from Savannah.

Meanwhile back at the school, my home economics teacher, Wilma Lay, encouraged us to choose our silver and crystal patterns and to start building our hope chests. Dutifully, I chose Lily of the Valley by Gorham and Early American Sandwich by Duncan from the line at Breckenridge Jewelry, located beside Henderson's café on Main Street. Then to place a seal on my choice, I purchased one glass for a dollar. Every girl needs hope, and I was full of hope and faith.

Next I began to pray that God would prepare a young man to be my mate for life.

God, you know who I need for a husband.

Will you place a love for you in his heart,

And instill a desire to go to church?

I suppose my prayer was a reflection of what I had seen in the men of Savannah. Many were not noted as loyal churchgoers. My own father was one who liked to use Sunday as a day to visit relatives in the Mt. Herman or Old Town communities.

I was beginning to form my opinions about a lot of things. I could see injustices and understand community issues. I recall hearing the townspeople talk about the details relating to how a young girl was shot and killed one night. Word spread that another girl, in a jealous rage, had shot her because she had dated her boy friend. But the boy friend testified that he was struggling with the deceased to try to get the gun away from her when she pulled the trigger and killed herself. The talk was that he married the other girl so that she could not testify at the trial.

His trial date came and he was acquitted. I listened as the town buzzed about the facts not coming out in that trial. I saw that no one was held responsible. How could that be?

As a young Christian woman, I thought, God knows and that's what counts. The real killer will have to stand before God one day. All sin has consequences and the penalty for sin is death—death in a hell of fire to be tormented forever. I wanted no part of that. Consequently, I felt sorry for the one who really had killed her if he or she had never asked for forgiveness.

The summers were extremely hot as they always had been in Savannah. The heat could suffocate, forcing its hot breath right in your face. Our enormous fan standing on a tall stand seemed at times to merely recycle the hot air of summer. The black asphalt and concrete under our window absorbed the heat and sent it spiraling to our upstairs living room window. And the top of Mr. Allen's building hardly helped when it channeled the hot air into our front bedroom window. Needing a cool breeze and finding none, I would run downstairs with my 10 cents and buy scraped ice sprinkled with lime or cherry syrup. Two young boys purchased a block of ice from Mr. Boaz at the Ice Plant and then scraped the ice to sell their treats. However, the heat from the sidewalk threatened to melt their newfound business venture.

My awareness of a world beyond my window continued to grow. It was in 1948 as I stood watching the river traffic that I heard the Jews now have a homeland. The survivors of the Holocaust now had a home. Bible prophecy was coming to pass. I became nervous, and the thoughts that flashed through my mind upset me. The Second Coming of Jesus was drawing nearer, and I had a lot of living to do first. I remember comforting myself by saying, "I am a Christian. I have an ever-present protector, a constant companion. I do not need to fear." Nonetheless, I wanted to grow up, have a home and children and a career.

In 1952 when I was a junior in high school, I remember hearing the music at the Baccalaureate. I wrote these words on the program when the choir sang, "Come Though Almighty King…Come, Holy Comforter, Come….Now rule in every heart." It was sad to see the seniors go. Some would go to the University of Tennessee in Knoxville, some to Memphis State, some to U.T. in Martin, some to work on parents' land, and some to work in the large cities while I continued going to classes with my cousins who were in the same grade—Margaret Ann Jerrolds, Reba Rich, John M. Neill, and Bobby Kerr.

April 1, 1953, was the day all of us had been waiting for. April Fools' Day. Our plans had been hatched in 1942 when we were in the third grade. In fact, our principal's daughter Cornelia had given us this plan, and through the years one cheerleader, Julia Thomas, reminded us as time drew near. We were to skip school on April Fools' Day 1953—the entire senior class. While we were finalizing our plans—either to go to Natural Bridge or to Pickwick—a senior homeroom teacher, Trudell Smith, came to the hillside where we had driven our cars and trucks and relayed his message, "Mr. Turman wants you to cancel your plans to skip school."

We had other plans.

Foolishly, when we stopped to buy snacks at a country grocery, the stop proved our mistake. Later Mr. Turman would track us to this store. He pulled up at Pickwick and directed Betty Jane, Cornelia, and me to get in his back seat and silently we drove the twelve miles back to high school. The next day each senior stood in line to enter the principal's office one at a time. I got through that questioning okay, but the next day I was called back to his office. What had I done now?

"Rich, if I recommend you for a scholarship to George Peabody College, would you accept it?" my principal questioned.

"Oh, yes."

I accepted this offer as being God's will for me. I had total faith that this door He had opened to me was a gift from heaven. My sister Verlene had gone to Memphis State, and like any sibling, I was excited to be able to go to another campus and chart my own course.

The winter slid into spring. Cornelia became Valedictorian; I was Salutatorian. My goal had been to be Number One, but being Number Two wasn't bad.

I wanted my Daddy to attend my graduation, but he wouldn't wear a necktie. He missed my speech and graduation. In my speech I quoted Alfred Lord Tennyson.

> "For I dipped into the future, Far as human eyes could see, Saw the vision of the world, And all the wonder that would be."

Just as I began my speech, I saw my brother H.C. enter the auditorium standing in the shadows of the balcony. I was so pleased he had made the trip to hear me. I ended my speech with "Nothing short of our best is good enough…The future belongs to us. New horizons await us."

I knew a college degree would take four years, but by going to summer school I could complete it in three years. There was something God wanted me to do so I would graduate from college as soon as possible. I strongly believed that God had placed this desire in my heart.

Questions to Consider:

1. How many churches are within a few miles of your home? Have you chosen one of them to be your church home?

2. Whom do you consider to be some of your sisters and brothers in Christ?

3. Do you consider God's will before making major decisions in your life?

A Bridge

From Childhood to Education and Life's Work

CHAPTER 6

Graduation Day and Off To George Peabody College

Once I found the bridge and stopped fording the streams of life, I found that I constantly had to fight to prevent myself from being tempted to wander back to the old habit of fording the stream. That's what happens when one starts taking the bridge. Genesis 3:15 describes that eternal struggle between the adversary and Jesus. Since I had been reared as a young lady of the church, I did not find myself lured to the "Bad Alley" type of detours from taking the bridge. Instead, my temptation was subtle—a desire to build something with my own hands-- a desire that could involve working independently of Jesus Christ, my bridge to perfect peace and to eternal life. Like Papa, I wanted to build a perfect life while I did it. Why not? I was an industrious, dedicated worker so when I was asked me to be editor of the annual my senior year, I worked to make it the best ever published, but I did not allow the extra load to interfere with my goal of reading a chapter in the Bible every night.

Nashvile was an interesting city with both culture and country music in the form of the grand Ole Opry. After graduation from George Peabody in Nashville, Principal Rex C. Turman offered me a teaching position at my high school alma mater. I would teach ninth-grade English, math and shorthand. Here I was so highly trained in all of the latest teaching methods and where would I be teaching—my old high school. I really wanted the job in Memphis City Schools—where everyone I knew so well would not be observing my performance; however, I took the position at Central High at $2,250 a year. Again my high school principal had come through for me and would influence my life.

As undercurrents of the Tennessee River flowed north…I wondered—Is this where God wants me to be? The river had always reminded me of far away places. For the time I contented myself by teaching at the high school and also teaching third graders in

Sunday school—one of whom was pianist Albert Bromley, who at this young age already showed great talent at playing the piano.

Even though I had trained to be an educator and had graduated from the Number One teacher-training institute in the country at that time, I continued to look for signs of what God would have me do with my life.

Settling in, I spruced up my bedroom in my family home. The room became pastel green with a few pieces of new furniture, including a Sonora television set with a black and white 21-inch screen—the first one that my family had ever owned.

After three years of being away at college, I returned to my post at the windows overlooking Courthouse Square. Something had changed. Now as a teacher all I saw were air conditioners sitting in windows sealing out the sounds that had given me clues as to the day-to-day news. Maybe this wasn't the same place I had left. I had changed and the town had changed too.

This returning to the old high school to teach proved to be an experience I will never forget. I was twenty years old and teaching Judy Falls, the daughter of my own former teacher. Knowing all of the family names in town, knowing the family's interest in education, and also knowing the stories of their lives even before classes began that fall proved to have both good and bad merits.

In a real twist to enrollment, in my 9th grade English class I had Jim Johnson and his brother-in-law, Benny Wallis, who was a senior and taking both 9th grade and 12th grade English at the same time due to an error in record keeping. The fifteen and eighteen-year-old combination was quite a load for a twenty- year- old teacher. To add to the mix I also taught three distant cousins of mine and to one, administered corporal punishment. Certainly I wanted to handle my own discipline issues and not let my old principal feel I couldn't handle whatever came up. The year was an odd assortment of the very best conditions working with and for Mr. Rex C. Turman combined with a bit of anxiety, because I wanted to demonstrate a bit of the George Peabody skills for my hometown neighbors. I wanted to become the best teacher in the school.

No doubt I worked harder than most new and old teachers at Central. The stakes for me were higher. After all, one does want to avoid making mistakes on the hometown turf.

One Sunday during that school year in 1957, I was singing in the choir beside Verlene when I spotted a young man wearing a gray suit accented with a pink necktie. He was seated in the right hand section of the pews. Handsome he was with his dark, wavy hair and tall, slender frame. Quick to inquire about our visitor I soon learned he had just completed four years in the U. S. Air Force. Good information but I thought little more about him until one Sunday a few weeks later he accompanied a friend to my house to play games around the kitchen table.

The three of us enjoyed the evening. I learned he worked in Memphis for an electric company. He told us about his landlady, Mrs. Hatsfield, who rented him a room in her boarding house in the Crosstown area of Memphis, near Cleveland and Poplar.

Meanwhile I focused on newfound friends in every area of my life, for I had developed strong bonds with many people that year. One dear friend, Mary E. Hitchcock, later became president of the Hardin County Historical Society. She, Jane Latimer, and Mrs. Phil Gillham answered my many questions that first year of teaching, as did other mentors, Mrs. W. B. Falls, Mrs. Raymond Shaw and Mrs. T. E. Miller.

The year ended as six college friends and I headed for Daytona Beach, Florida. My previous college roommate, Judy Garner, and I had planned this vacation two years earlier. I wanted my summer school roommate, Kitty Simpson, to go with us but her sister Jean went in her place. We worked on our tans and discussed our futures.

Upon returning home, I decided I needed to use my business minor. After placing an ad in the Commercial Appeal, I received a call from Furniture by Fleming's owner, Partee Fleming. He asked me what salary I needed, and I told him I had to make $250 a month in order to move to Memphis. He hired me on the spot. Now I could give my resignation at Central High. There had to be an easier way to make a living than by teaching students who were related to me, or who were in my Sunday school room at church. Also, I needed time to place some age difference between my students and me. A bookkeeping job was the perfect solution.

Questions to Consider:

1. Do you sometimes find that your own self sufficiency is your enemy?

2. How can you, in your situation, become more dependent upon God?

3. Do you pray before making job changes?

CHAPTER 7

Betty Joyce And The Man From The U.S. Air Force

Drexel, my handsome young Air Force veteran, took a job with the Civil Service at the Post Office in Memphis. He continued to call me and when both of us stayed in the city on the weekends, we attended church services and ate Sunday dinner together. Our favorite places were the Rebel on Summer Avenue, Britlings on Poplar, or the Cotton Bowl on Parkway.

Soon new friendships developed at the furniture store. Outgoing and friendly, Frances Hall came to work at Furniture by Fleming. Now we had two females in the building. Frances, one unique saleslady in action, had two daughters, Billie, an actress in high school plays, and Judy, still in elementary school. Frances, with her deep religious convictions had quite a strong influence upon my life.

As I became closer to Drexel, I noted that he had a big heart and a deep concern for people with disabilities. Then I learned he had a younger brother whose brain surgeries had not produced the results intended, thus leaving him legally blind with only five percent of his vision remaining. Undoubtedly this brother's illness had influenced Drexel to develop deep thoughts and convictions concerning people with disabilities.

I also noticed that Drexel was drawn to music. When the heater in his gray Dodge went out that winter, we continued to ride in it because Drexel's car had a radio. When we became so cold we could not tolerate the cold any longer, we took my car with no radio. Always he had the radio turned on, and at any moment he might burst out in song as we rode down the road.

I began to really look at this man I was spending so much time with. I certainly had moved beyond the fact that he was handsome with his green eyes the color of shallow spring water. When he smiled at me, I noticed that one of his front teeth slightly overlapped the one next to it, only adding character to his All-American face. His smile exhibited friendliness with caution.

To add to my picture of Drexel were the years he had spent in the United States Air Force. First he had trained in this country in Texas and Oklahoma, then going via San Francisco to Korea where he spent many a frigid night on guard duty. For a girl who had not had so many adventures, Drexel's military history made him even more appealing.

Possibly because of this military life and also because he had been the eldest of his four surviving siblings, Drexel was, for the most part, quite serious mannered. I, on the other hand, could appear fun loving and carefree. These opposites were attracting each other like strong magnets.

As I had pictured my future husband, I had pictured a young man with a college education and one who had character. Of course, I had other criteria that this man of my dreams had to meet, but Drexel had met one prerequisite on that list. Now we were down to the last two very serious factors that we had to address.

As for the college degree requirement, Drexel had been serving his country when I was going to college. I had to remember that. I also had to look at the score he had made on his Civil Service exam. He was indeed a bright young man and an industrious one at that.

One night after eating barbecue at Berretta's, Drexel and I were listening to the words of a popular song. The lyrics portrayed giving someone a rainbow to wear on her finger and then going out and buying her the moon. Drexel sang along with the lyrics when suddenly he became quiet and pensive.

"Betty, you have never mentioned the fact that I have been married before."

"I think that you are probably a better person for having been married to Bettie Lou," I replied. (His wife of eleven months had tragically died in the hospital following minor surgery. She was graduated a year before me at my high school and her sister had been my sister's roommate at Memphis State.)

He said nothing, but our relationship deepened after that night.

The problem with the former marriage and the lack of college degree had become the reasons Mother did not want me to date Drexel. She instead wanted to me date the young dentist who was renting the office in our Rich building. One night the dentist asked me for a date. I accepted. We rode across Pickwick Dam to eat a steak at Counce, Tennessee. The entire evening my thoughts were on Drexel.

In the following days, two things occurred. I met a person important to my teaching career, and I knew for certain Drexel was the man for me. First, at work, a true Southern gentleman walked in to make a payment on his furniture. As I wrote the receipt, we talked. I learned he was the assistant superintendent of Memphis City Schools. Immediately, I volunteered that I had taught one year before moving to Memphis. As I wrote the receipt, he continued to measure me and as he walked away, he said, "Betty, if you ever decide to go back to teaching, just let me know." It was unknown to me at that time why my path crossed with Morgan Christian, but in the future I would clearly see.

After the date with the dentist, I now knew how much I really cared for Drexel. We went to church and ate our Sunday meals. We both knew without voicing it that we belonged together.

To this day, we do not remember a formal, "Will you marry me?" We do remember that we simply began to say, "When we get married...." My only request was that he complete the test required to enroll for classes at Memphis State and use his GI Bill to obtain a degree. He did just that.

One day Drexel asked me if I wanted to select my rings. At that time Brodnax, Memphis' most reputable jewelry store, was located on Main Street near the Mississippi River. My selection was a white gold set with one large diamond and six small diamonds—four on the wedding band and one on either side of the large stone. In 1957 the cost of these rings was $320, and Drexel agreed to pay for them in 12 monthly payments. Words cannot express the emotions that I felt when Drexel placed that engagement ring on my finger. We were in Overton Park and the sunlight picked up the light in that ring and sparkled like no diamond I had ever seen before.

Like many brides of that time, I followed the schedule in the bridal book for planning the wedding. I selected a long white wedding dress at Goldsmith's for $80. That was a lot of money in that year. All of the accessories were chosen. Then selection of the invitations followed. Finally, on June 1, 1958, my picture was published on the society section of the Sunday Commercial Appeal.

On June 22, 1958, at 4:00 p.m., we were married in our church at Union and McLean. Drexel was twenty-six years old and I was twnety-two. After the wedding we went to our apartment to change into our "going away" clothes. Drexel wore new pants and a blazer he had bought at Bonds behind Lowensteins East on Highland. I chose a bright deep pink dress—pink was my dad's favorite color. We were now ready for our New Orleans honeymoon.

We had leased a newly constructed apartment near Memphis State campus. In all of the United States, there probably was not a more enviable location to live than Memphis, for in 1958 the lyrics of the songs of Elvis Presley were on the lips of everyone in the country. Besides that, other great singers like Johnny Cash had recorded at Memphis' Sun Records. So, it was Drexel and I living in Memphis on the Mississippi River—the best place to be.

Soon we began to see some bits of personality we had failed to notice earlier. To reveal the differences in the Rich and Hendon upbringing, I relate the story of the evening when I stopped at the TG&Y to buy some sewing items I needed. By the time I arrived home, Drexel had called Fleming Furniture Store to see if I had left on schedule. I was not used to this smothering. We Riches considered everything to be going as scheduled until we heard something to the contrary. My parents were not afraid of thunder, lightning, storms, but the Hendons feared dark clouds and storms. Both of our families had strong bonds of love for each other, but I began to notice the security they found in their tight circle. Also, our family had not had as much tragedy in the small family circle. Drexel's brother's brain tumor and later his young wife's tragic death had undoubtedly made him much more apprehensive about all sorts of phenomena that might cause harm to me or to both of us.

As with any young couple, we also began to notice all of the differences in each other's upbringing. With the Hendons you never had to wonder where you stood with them, for they told you exactly where they stood. In my family, however, we might have the same thoughts, but we would be careful not to voice them for fear of hurting each other's feelings.

We were learning about these little idiosyncrasies in each other, and soon we celebrated our one-year anniversary. We had been married almost a year when I caught the flu, or so it seemed. After all of the tests were in, I learned that my flu was really a pregnancy! Drexel was elated. Betty was sick. Every morning for a full three months, I could not keep anything on my stomach. Crackers eaten before rising did not help in the least. Drexel suggested that I try eating grapes for breakfast since I could not tolerate the aroma of frying bacon. Mornings were awful. Afternoons were fine.

Together we chose the name for our baby. If we had a boy, we agreed he should be named Barry Clift. If we had a girl, we had a list of ten names on which we would come to a conclusion.

Questions to Consider:

1. Did you or do you now see God in the changes of plans in your past?

2. Could it be that God uses marriage to trim the rough edges off the personalities of marriage partners?

A Bridge
To The Next Generation

CHAPTER 8

Barry Clift: A Compact Bundle Of Life And Joy

December 25, 1959, was a day of miracles. My Christmas gift was wrapped in white—no red bow—just a simple white blanket and under this warm blanket was a warm bundle dressed in yellow.

As I looked at the gift that God had given to Drexel and me, my eyes scanned a tiny head with a stock of black hair, closed eyes and round cheeks. I loved that warm, cuddly baby that lay in my arms.

As I looked at him I wanted God to envelope him in spiritual protection:

"Reverence for God gives a man deep strength; his children have a place of refuge and safety. " Proverbs 14:26 TLB

Furthermore, I wanted our son to have a special heritage that only God can give. I certainly didn't want to be guilty of taking calcium before his birth, and then after his birth not give him a spiritual heritage.

"His children shall be honored everywhere, for good men's sons have a special heritage." Psalm 112:2 TLB

Housing on campus in Vet village became available for $23 per month; we were pleased to move before the birth of our son.

When Barry was only four weeks old, Drexel encouraged me to start taking courses for my Masters Degree while we were still living on campus. Then he went one step further, he suggested that I major in guidance counseling, with a minor in English and Curriculum and Instruction. We had talked about all of this many times, and I agreed wholeheartedly that this is the way I should continue with my educational endeavor. Without my knowledge, this new degree would play a major role in my future career.

In 1959 our family added a life and one was taken away. My dear grandfather Poney died a painful death of cancer the year our son Barry was born. Barry would continue the Rich family line, even as a Hendon.

Barry was full of energy and mischief. At an early age he was happiest in motion. As long as his Daddy would jump him up and down, he would laugh contentedly no matter how tired he had become.

One family story we have repeated over and over occurred when Barry was only six months old. He went to stay with his Grandmother Rich for four days. She placed quilts and pillows on the floor by her double bed and was content that this would be the best place for Barry to sleep. That way she would not have to worry that he would roll off the bed. The following morning when she turned over and looked down, the baby had disappeared. She rushed through the house and checked to see if the front door was locked. Everything was as she had left it the night before except her grandson was missing. Finally having looked every other place, she looked under the bed. There was baby Barry sound asleep on the hardwood floor. Grandmother was weak from fright, but her grandson was fine.

By the time Barry was nine months old, it was evident that I needed to go back to work. We needed an income for us to live on while Drexel completed his college work. I remembered the assistant superintendent I had met while working at Fleming Furniture, so I contacted the Memphis City School system. Soon I was hired to teach English at Southside High School, but their enrollment did not reach expectations and I was soon sent to Overton High School to teach 11th grade English.

Being the new teacher, I didn't stay at Overton long either. Soon I was placed at Memphis Technical High School to teach 12th-grade college prep English and typing for the principal, W.A. Bourne. The parents and students in this neighborhood were very supportive of the teachers; there was no problem in the area of discipline. This school was truly a good place for me to settle in the Memphis City Schools, because the students were eager to learn—one of my precocious students, Roland Pittman, won a full scholarship to MIT. I hoped that I had taught him how to write a term paper, how to express himself well in both written and verbal communication, how to use the parts of speech, and how to enjoy poetry and the dramatic works of Shakespeare.

I wanted to make a difference in the lives of my students by challenging them to use their potential to the maximum—that making 94 on a test isn't good enough if they have the ability to make 100. I also wanted to build up those with less ability to experience the joy of performing on their level, and I wanted to motivate them to achieve so that they would experience the joy of success. I wanted my students to ask questions, do research, study hard, and achieve the true joy of learning, because I knew from personal experience in high school that one teacher could make a difference. I did not care what salary I make—I wanted to make the classroom an exciting place. I wanted to make poetry like The Raven by Poe come alive—Shakespeare's characters live on the stage—to make the lives of my students come alive as well. Salary wasn't that important, but making a difference was.

I wanted to live out the verse that I read in the Bible: **"A wise teacher makes learning a joy . . . ." Proverbs 15:2 TLB**

When Drexel graduated from Memphis State, we thought we were moving to Marion, Indiana, in pursuit of employment. However, a rapid turn of events in Drexel's favor took place and he was asked to fill a vacant position in Rehabilitation Medicine at Kennedy Veteran's Hospital in Memphis. His work would be restoring veterans to good health.

When Barry was almost four years old, I completed my Masters work at Memphis State. A difficult course, Statistics, was behind me, and I had completed my practicum in guidance under our Tech guidance counselor, Margaret Kelly, and had completed my written and oral exams.

As I was completing my Masters, ready for a new phase of life, my brother and his wife were getting a divorce. Nonetheless he flew to Memphis in his own plane for my graduation. He joined Mother who wore her pillbox hat, blue dress and white gloves.

Fortunately for his parents and ultimately for him, Barry was good at entertaining himself. He alternated playing on his swing set to his tricycle to his toy chest in the bedroom. He loved animals, and we got him a pup named Pip based on the character from the Charles Dickens novel, *Great Expectations*, which I was teaching at Tech High School.

On November 22, 1963, our librarian, Mrs. Francis Martin, brought me news that I could not comprehend. President John F. Kennedy had been fatally shot. He was dead! The whole country had to process this information. None of us could believe what we had heard! The news stunned me. Our president had been assassinated. Where was the security in Texas? I received the news as I stood in front of a 10th-grade English class. A hush of disbelief hung over the room as we ached for our country. I could not complete the assignment. I shall never forget that day.

The following day our four-year-old Barry turned the television on for his usual cartoons and all of the channels covered the news of the president's death. There were no cartoons. We sat glued to the television news, leaving only for an appointment and then returning to hear this sad story that would undoubtedly become an important turning point in our American History.

After this event that upset everyone locally and nationally, Drexel and I began to think about the need to buy a home that would be located in the best possible school district for Barry who had completed kindergarten. Soon we found the right place and made the move just in time for him to enter the first grade.

I continued to teach at Tech High, and Drexel was employed at the Veteran's Hospital which now had a new campus with its move from Park to Jefferson near the Baptist Hospital.

Meanwhile back in Savannah, Mother reported there was quite a bit of excitement when the grandson of a resident announced he was going to compile a history about his African American ancestors, Alex and Queen Haley. Week after week, there would be new information in the Savannah Courier. All of my life I had heard much about the Stringtown section of Savannah, but now every time I talked with Mother there was something new revealed about the African American population that had grown up just across town from me. I had been an eagle eye over Main Street, but apparently, there had been much that I had missed. Soon the book *Roots* would be written by Haley, and I would learn even more about the African Americans of Savannah.

On April 4, 1968, I was at a faculty meeting with W. A. Bourne, when Drexel called our school and asked to speak with Mr. Bourne. He reported that Dr. Martin Luther King, Jr. had been assassinated at the Lorraine Motel and that some areas of downtown Memphis had been set on fire.

Mr. Bourne dismissed the teacher training session and told us to go home immediately. As I walked out the side door to where my Plymouth was parked, I looked up at the sky at the black smoke clouds. The sound of the sirens was deafening; traffic was snarled. Tech High was located only 12 blocks from Main Street where the burning and looting took place. The whole city was in a state of chaos and panic!

Not just a few buildings were burning, but whole sections had been set afire. To say I was scared and uneasy as I worked my way across traffic trying to head toward the east is an understatement so silently I sent up a prayer of protection.

I recalled that in the morning newspaper I had read about the visit of Martin Luther King, Jr. to Memphis. He had come to settle a strike in the city's sanitation department.

Questions to Consider:

1. Do you feel that today's children are honored everywhere as in Psalm 112: 2 TLB

2. What does it mean to honor a child?

3. Do you have a day or night in your life when you were frightened for yourself and your whole community?

Building The Teacher

Mentoring Bridge To The Future

Chapter 9

Memphis, April 1968: Smoke Clouds In The Rearview Mirror

As I drove, my mind was a jumble. First I was thinking of Drexel and Barry. I was thinking of how dangerous it was for me to be driving during this period of danger as whoever was responsible for the assassination and for setting the fires was undoubtedly darting through streets trying to get away from police. I also thought about the day in assembly at Tech when Mr. Bourne had introduced the first African American student to our previously all-white student body. He stated that the Board of Education had chosen our school for integration, that he did not expect to have any trouble in school, and that he knew the student body would accept our new student. We had not disappointed him.

Driving now, I somehow knew that this era of my teaching career was coming to a close. After this night of fright, I knew Drexel would suggest the time had come for me to move my teaching to the suburbs near to our home. Being down in the inner city so far from our home really made no sense. Barry needed me to be able to run by his school in the evenings. I realized that and I knew that I would soon be making a move.

As I drew closer to our house and the noise of the sirens faded, I recalled the year that Mr. Bourne had selected me to teach the first vocational education class at Tech. The State Department of Education had vocational funds allocated to help high school students with training for job placement after graduation. Within this Vocational Office Occupations class I taught advanced typing, business English, and office machines. Subsequently, I had enrolled at MSU and finished all the requirements to be certified by the State Department in the area of Vocational Office Education. At that time the area was so new there was no number coding on my certification. I was certainly ahead of the times.

I also applied to teach part time at Memphis State and was assigned classes teaching typing and shorthand in night school and in summer school.

During my eight years at Tech, I felt the love that radiated from my students. I cherished the fact that the annual yearbook of 1968 was dedicated to me and to Mrs. Edna Norwood, the school secretary and bookkeeper. I was proud of the accomplishments of my homeroom: first place in PTA membership drive; first place in PTA attendance at Open House; second place in Thanksgiving Basket Drive; third place in Christmas Basket Drive; and seven winners in the Hall of Fame.

As well as reminiscing about my time at inner city Tech High, I could also feel that my life had come full circle in one important area. Having lived a somewhat sheltered life in small town Savannah, then attending prestigious George Peabody School at Vanderbilt, I had not known much about being excluded, or living in poverty. Even as I was angry that through my rearview mirror I could see images of parts of the city of Memphis on fire, I knew that after working in the inner city and working in a school where there had been successful integration of races, I had a better understanding of the confusion that was occurring in our downtown than many people who lived on the outskirts of Memphis or who were hearing about the burning of the city on national television. Certainly, a whole race of people had seen their hopes dashed on this day.

Finally I was safe inside my house. The remainder of the night we listened to the news of the death of Dr. Martin Luther King, Jr. and of the burning of Memphis.

For weeks the city was under curfew. This was a time of extreme unrest in our city. Nightly, we watched the evening news and saw the gutted, charred buildings in the downtown area of Memphis.

Questions to Consider:

1. What skills has God given you to help calm yourself and others in time of crisis?

2. Has God given you a love for people that you didn't have when He was not in your life?

3. If so, what are you doing to show this love for others?

4. Are there other ways that that come to mind that you could increase your ministry in this area?

CHAPTER 10

The Dramatic 1960s In The Field Of Education

In 1968 I began teaching at Wooddale High School where the principal, D. Winton Simmons, was wonderfully receptive to hearing our teacher voices as he directed our school. The 1960s had been a "dramatic" period in the field of education, for at the college level there were almost daily sit-ins and demonstrations; at the high schools, the students were not only being touched by the turbulent Vietnam War years, the court-ordered busing and integration, but also by the introduction to illicit drug usage. Add all of those elements to the fact that the city of Memphis continued to reel under the burden of being the site of the assassination of Dr. Martin Luther King, Jr.

At Wooddale High the majority of the students were all-American wholesome young people whose lives revolved around their class work, the Friday night games, band and glee club. However, a few in this area where money was more prevalent than it had been in the Tech High community were now experimenting with drugs, especially marijuana. Just beyond the school yard, out in the shadows were hatred and ugly elements that could create destruction for our kids.

Conflict arose in the student body, and at times pep rallies aroused bitter feelings between black and white students. Teachers now had to police the pep sessions and during the school day had to monitor the restrooms and keep constant vigilance in the hallways. Occasionally teachers, both men and women, were called upon to step into the middle of a fight to break it up. These duties were, for the most part, new to the field of education. Where previously we had taken a casual attitude toward such necessary surveillance, we now scheduled it into the day's work. Times indeed were changing. Sadly, some of the activities young high school students had previously enjoyed had to be curtailed indefinitely.

To top it all, the parents' attitudes were also changing. Most remarkably many parents could not believe their children were involved in experimenting with drugs. They would not work with the faculty at school to help their children address the fact that drugs were ruining their lives. Many parents worked long hours to provide a better environment for their families. They then had no time to give close supervision to their children after school and at night.

Television programming began to change and give its viewers more of what it demanded—loud music, sexually explicit scenes and violence. As our appetites grew, we wanted more money, more cars, and more clothes. In short, our society had fallen into the pains of acquisition.

Students now drove cars to school. This created the need for money for gasoline, insurance, car repairs, and maintenance. Peer pressure had always been a factor with young people, but that too changed in its serious consequences. Where earlier the pressure had been to climb the town's water tower on Halloween night, now the pressure was to engage in drug use or sexual activity that would, without fail, affect the life of the student forever.

I remember a story that my minister told about a teacher—it hit home with me. He told about Miss Eva who was a teacher in both church and school. Many lives had been changed by Miss Eva, who never married. One day she was asked if she thought that she was planting seeds in the lives of her students, because so many had become ministers, missionaries, and true Christian laymen. She responded that a teacher is not planting seeds; she is doing something more important that that. God's word will have an impact in their lives at one time or another and just explode.

I thought of teaching as turning on a light bulb. When I was teaching Sunday school, I tried to breathe warmth and life into the events and characters in the Bible, but I was fully aware that the Holy Spirit had to touch the heart and make God's word come alive—being alive in Christ was a wonderful feeling.

After years of teaching at church, I began to understand more about the verse in Matthew 17:20 when it speaks of moving a mountain. Mountains personify any huge problem in our lives—sickness, death, loss of job, financial problems, depression, and strained family relationships are only a few examples. Jesus gives us the one word we need—FAITH. As his children we only need so little faith to work our way through these problems. Every person has problems, but each reacts differently to them.

It is no surprise that Jesus went often to the mountains to pray. A mountain symbolized the highest point on earth where He could be alone and talk with his Father when he was physically exhausted from his day's work and teaching. He was the MASTER TEACHER.

My desire as a teacher was to tell others how to know the storm maker and the peace speaker like the song by Geron Davis. I wanted my students to find the BRIDGE.

Questions to Consider:

1. Has God shown you that children who look and sometimes act like adults, cannot handle adult situations?

2. Can you see areas in our modern culture where we adults are introducing or suggesting sin to our youth of today?

3. If so, how could you be a ray of light to counter those suggestions? Perhaps steering that child to a wholesome role model?

WHAT I HAVE LEARNED IN MY YEARS WITH CHILDREN:

"Train up a child in the way he should go; and when he is old, he will not depart from it." Proverbs 22:6

How can we save the children in this country from the outpouring of evil that is intent upon winning them over? My years as a principal and teacher reveal a few truths that I feel are worth recording:

1. Know that sin is often appealing and enticing to the young. There is a lure involved in winning over our sons and daughters.
2. The appeal through some music—the lyrics as well as the beat—is sexually seductive and forceful in encouraging violence, hatred and unnatural acts against men, women, people in authority, and even children.
3. The whole world feeds our children a humanistic philosophy…if it feels good, do it.

4. We as parents and as a nation seem no longer intent on building character in our young. We do not follow through on what we say we will do.
5. We as parents and as a nation are not fostering responsibility in our young.
6. We are not promoting the family unit. We say, "Life is short—if you stop loving a spouse, by all means, leave."
7. Children are pawns in these broken homes—with this year's partner being one person and next year's partner, another.
8. Consequently, many of our children do not know security and stability in any area of their lives. A simple reading of traditional children's literature like "The Three Pigs" is too close to the fears they live with daily. They do not know who will be "there" for them.
9. Even sixth-grade students require constant supervision in all areas of the school building.
10. Children have little to look forward to, for they have already experienced too much of adult life. They are allowed to enter adult situations, which they cannot handle.
11. We cannot expect our children to grow strong in ways of the Lord when there are few role models and when there is very little day-to-day training.
12. Older people are busy traveling and enjoying their retirement years when, on occasion, their wealth of knowledge and wisdom might be shared in a mentoring situation with the young.
13. Children usually know exactly what is going on at home, in the neighborhood and at school—all of the immorality among teachers, neighboring adults and peers.
14. When children are not steered toward wholesome role models, they gravitate to other areas such as toward the often-corrupt rock music and movie idol worlds, which do want their attention and their money.
15. Few children's television viewing is monitored.
16. Few children's computer habits are scrutinized or blocked out.
17. Toys do not take the place of having the parents' time and attention.
18. Today there seems to be no place where it is acceptable to say "No" to a child. Some parents and caregivers are under

the gun of being so careful not to abuse that they are not disciplining their children at all.

19. Children seek the security of boundaries and guidelines.
20. Children seek human relationships---a pat on the back, a smile, and a kind word.
21. When Jesus Christ is in the home, parents are present too.

WHEN THE HOME HAS FAILED, THE TEACHER HAS THE OPPORTUNITY TO FILL IN THE GAPS:

The teacher/educator is often in a position to observe the reaction of students who have proper role models in the home environment.

The teacher has the vantage point opportunity to see how the child acts upon what parents and the church taught them.

The teacher watches as the child steps out and makes choices, deals with peer pressure, and reacts to taunts and teases, to swearing, to prejudice, to patriotism, to references to God, and to vulgarity.

The teacher watches as the child observes and reacts to poverty, to achievement, to doing their best work, to authority, to respect of elders, to the chronically or acutely ill, and to the opposite sex.

Teachers observe habits that could become lifelong—tardiness, absenteeism, lack of structure, procrastination– also to being confined when the person is an outdoors type, to commercialism, to having the "right" home address, to appreciation or the lack thereof, and to creative activities that put the individual stamp on a work.

Teachers see choices in reading materials and choices of television shows and movies viewed.

Teachers wonder as they see fear, results of war zones in the homes, evidence of legal authority in their lives—the police and the courts, property damage and vandalism, evidence of stalking and jealousies, and dealings with retaliation.

Teachers hold their collective breath as the child moves through bodily changes---bridging from adolescence to adulthood, making college and career choices, learning to drive an automobile, and discovering self-identity.

Teachers watch as the children expand their worldview, see beyond their local community, accept their civic duties, and discern what rights they have in this world.

Heritage

Maternal grandparents, Clara and Oscar Solomon
with first child, Blanche, 1907

Poney's father, William Frank Rich,
Union Soldier

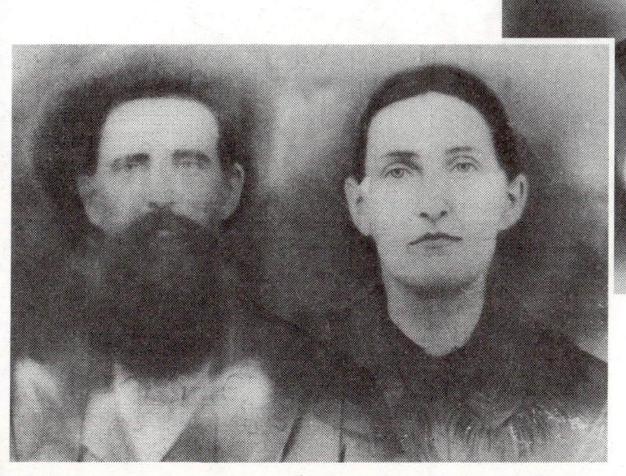

Confederate soldier, Alfred Alexander Neill
with wife, Sarah Jane Young

Family

Betty's grandparent's and father: Poney Rich, Clyde, Oma, daisy, and Gladys.

Betty's father, Clyde "Cubby" Rich, 1940

Betty's mother, Zelma Rich, 1993

Betty's sister Verlene Rich,
the bread lady
1950

Betty's brother, H.C.
Rich, 1946

Betty's husband, Drexel Hendon, USAF, Korea

Betty, 1958

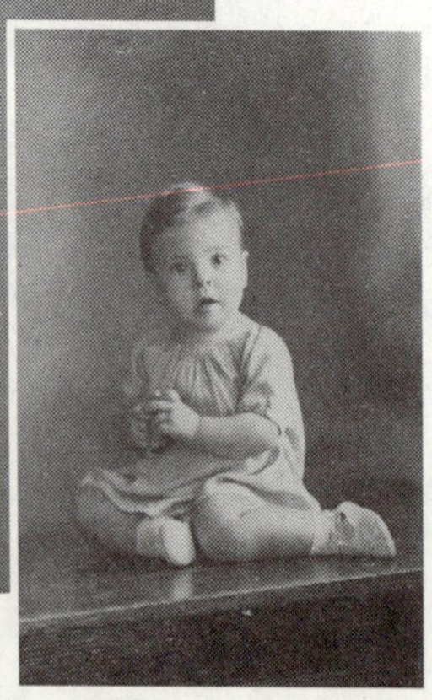

Betty, Age 1

The Hendon Family

Barry, Age 4

Betty and Barry, Trafalgar Square, 1980

History

The Patterson Place

Betty, Principal of Manor Lake Elementary, National Teachers' Day
USPS officials adopted the school

Betty after Bible Study, eating with the "Lunch Bunch," seated Ginger Waugh, Nell Hawkins, guest Barbara Childers, Becky Sibley, Betty Johnson, and Kathleen Daniel

Betty and Verlene at Rich Family Reunion, 1995, Pickwick, TN

Betty with high school classmates at luncheon in Nashville, TN
L to R: Betty Carlock, Rita Irwin, Julia Adkisson, Margaret Rich, Betty, Mary Jene Reynolds, and Helen Noffsinger

Betty and Drexel at Barry's Animal Hospital with her college roomn
Judy , and her husband, Dr. Virgil Crowder, Jr., Barry's fellow Rotar

CHAPTER 11

Guiding A Child At Home
While Leading Children At School

At home I was seeing Barry deal with some of the same things I witnessed at school. Fortunately for our family, he was an obedient child and had the understanding that all activity has its consequences. He enjoyed playing all sports and serving as manager of the track team. He delighted many with his magic tricks which he had worked to perfection. Area people even hired him to perform at their children's birthday parties, and he volunteered to perform at the local library. He was gentle and kind with children, animals and the elderly.

When he was 12 or 13 years old, he was reading a book about John F. Kennedy. He came flying down the hall from his room, "Mom, Mom, will you make the same deal with me that Kennedy's father made with his son?"

"What in the world are you talking about?"

"Well, Kennedy's Dad told him that he would give him $1,000 if he would not smoke or drink until he was 21 years old. How about it?" he pressed; "Will you make the same deal with me?"

I considered what he was saying and decided it certainly had merits. "You know I think that's a pretty good contract. Yes, Barry, I will make that deal with you, but I want to add two other items because your generation is different. I'll agree if you add abstaining from sex and drugs to the list. Do you agree?"

He agreed.

When Barry had completed his middle school years, he knew he wanted to become a veterinarian. This decision and the fact that he was excelling at his school work prompted us to enroll him at the Memphis University School, a college prep school, where he graduated Magna Cum Laude in 1977. From there he headed to the University of Tennessee where there was an established School of Veterinary Medicine.

The following is a letter I wrote to him on his 18th birthday:

A Letter to my Son on his Eighteenth Birthday:

Barry, you are a joy to share our home with this Christmas Season. I am so proud of your 4.0 grade average, but I am much prouder that you do not drink, or smoke, or experiment with drugs.

What a well-rounded individual you have become! And what a bright mind you have. Now your teasing is something else. I'm afraid I must say that is definitely something that you have inherited from your "Mom."

I hear your car coming in the drive now, and I am proud that you came in before 12:00 p.m. (even on your birthday)...it is 11:30 to be exact.

As your Dad said last night, "He is the bright spot in my life."

Forgive me for the times when you are away at college, and I get scared of life's influences on your character. Always stay true to God. You shall prosper and have peace, joy everlasting, and life eternal.

Love,
Mom
December 21, 1977

In 1980, after three years of study in pre-vet courses, he was accepted to enter the School of Veterinary Medicine; we asked him if he wanted to accompany us on our summer vacation.

"Where are you going?"

"England."

That was a trip he could not turn down. And what a delightful trip it was. We went to Wimbledon for the championship tennis tournament, took the traditional tours of London's famous places, and attended a couple of plays, including *The Mousetrap*. Then we rode the train to Cambridge and Stratford-on-Avon. We even found some ties to the Hendon family name at Hendon Station near London.

While on the train, I looked out the window and reflected on the fulfillment of the agreement that Barry and I had made when he was thirteen:

Only weeks earlier, Barry had reminded me that I was nearing pay-up time on our pact. He told me, "Mom, I have just one more year before I can claim the thousand dollars. I have kept my end of the contract."

As he spoke, I thought these words to myself. Thank you, Lord. This is the best trade I could have made with my son. Thank you for allowing him to read that book which placed this idea in his mind. Thank you for helping me to make a wise decision.

A few weeks later, Barry came to me again.

"Mom, I've been looking at some stock, Japan Fund; if you want to buy it for $700 now, it will be worth a thousand when I am twenty-one."

I purchased the stock in his name and placed it in a safe place. I was well pleased with this arrangement. Looking out the window of the train I thought of all of these conversations and enjoyed every one.

Our little family knew this trip would be one upon which we would comment and reflect for the rest of our lives. The three of us laughed and reminisced, totally relaxed and focused on our enjoyment of each other. As I looked at Barry, I saw a dreamer like his Grandfather Hendon and a doer like his Grandfather Rich. What a combination! He clinched his jaws and set high goals for himself, and he usually achieved them. He was not afraid of work and the busier he was, the happier he was. Budgeting came easily—he allocated his funds to make them go the farthest. While on this trip he revealed to us that he dreamed of building his own animal clinic and hospital. While we cautioned him of the overhead, we believed he would succeed.

His head of hair he had inherited from Papa Solomon, but his hairy chest and legs he had inherited from his Grandfather Rich. We laughingly say that the men in the Hendon family have slick legs—no hair. He has his father's rounded face, dark brown hair and "my" dark brown eyes with olive skin that tans a golden brown. He has broad shoulders and a slim 34-inch waistline. His 180 lbs. are well distributed on his 6'1" frame.

On this trip we were once again reminded that Barry loves to tease. Together the three of us remembered how he had a special way to tease his mother and his dad. For me, he enjoyed catching me in a serious mood and giving me a flippant answer to my serious question. When he was a young teen, he decided he wanted to sit with his friends in the church balcony each Sunday during the sermon. To assure myself that he was indeed listening to the sermon, I began the ritual of asking him a question about the sermon or the singing or something significant that had occurred that morning. On occasion, in order to get a reaction from me, he would purposely give a wrong answer and then howl in laughter at my dismayed facial expression. When he had enjoyed the moment to the maximum he would then tell me the answer I was searching for. Barry's teasing had won.

For his Dad, he reserved the pleasure of aggravating him by provoking a wrestling session or playing a trick on Drexel. One of his favorites was stepping on the toe of his Dad's socks in order to cause him to walk out of them. How many times did I hear in a voice that was less than convincing, "Now, Bear, don't do that."

As a mother who has lived more years than her son, I could see how this sense of humor would serve this talented son of ours. Life could become less cumbersome with such a humorous approach.

"Train up a child in the way he should go, and when he is old, he will not depart from it." Proverbs 22:6

Questions to Consider:

1. Do you program your child to fail? Of course, no one sets out to do so, but it happens. When a parent says, "He is so bad; he fights all of the boys in our neighborhood, he is a born fighter" that parent is programming her son to fulfill her expectations of him. Listen to your comments about your child. Do you see that your child fulfills what you expect of him?

2. Are you purposely setting yourself up as the role model in your child's life? If you are not, he or she will choose someone else to be that role model. The choice could be detrimental to his or her development.

3. Can you think of a specific pact you might make with a child in your home or in your community regarding preserving that child's high moral standards in a given area?

4. Have you remembered to tell a young person in your home or church or community that you are proud of the way that person conducts himself in the world?

5. How is "training a child" different from "feeding and clothing" a child?

BUILDING THE BRIDGE TO THE NEXT GENERATION

Everyone has a child. There is a child in the family or a child in the neighborhood. With each child comes the opportunity to impart truth—that includes imparting truth to the neighbor's child who sits in your flower garden even as you read!

1. Self awareness and self image engendered into and unfolding in a child—all come from the perceptions and understandings that start at home.
2. At home and in the neighborhood a child learns where he or she fits in and how he or she can contribute to this unit. Do I have chores I must do? Do I take and not give? Do I serve?
3. At home one learns what love is and how to express it.
4. At home one starts the disciplined life. All of the structure a child will need to work and live in the world that says, "You must be on time, with neat appearance, and you must fit your success story into a certain time frame without breaking laws."
5. At home a child learns to be generous. Who am I when I am with other children? How do I share my possessions?
6. At home and in the close circle of family and friends a child learns to use money effectively. What is worthy of his spending?
7. At home a child learns to love and preserve creation.
8. At home one learns to care about others–to invent ways to make life's journey more enjoyable for those who cannot help themselves.
9. At home a child learns where the boundaries lie. What is too much? What is too much television? What is too much candy? Too much visiting with friends?
10. At home as a child hears adults talking she learns there are consequences to every behavior. Playing with clay is fun, but when clay is ground into the carpet, the carpet is ruined. What happens when I don't look and run out into the street?
11. At home one learns what behavior is appropriate for specific occasions.
12. At home a child learns what she likes and what she dislikes.

13. At home one learns to honor and respect. One learns what is worthy of celebration.
14. At home a child develops traditions that will go with that child throughout life.
15. At home a child forms his first thoughts about death and dying. He learns what illness is really serious and what can usually be treated.
16. At home one learns about instant gratification and about waiting.
17. At home we learn who our ancestors were and how their lives relate to our own.

Crossing The Bridge

When A Generation Comes Full Circle

CHAPTER 12

H.C. Goes To Heaven

As a child H .C. had been more docile than his sisters, Betty and Verlene. Our H.C. had dark eyes, dark hair, and pug nose-- no aquiline nose for him. He stood six feet tall with 220 lbs. and was an extrovert with a sweet disposition.

In 1954 my brother, H.C. Rich, completed Basic Training in the United States Air Force in San Antonio. By 1955 doctors in Cheyenne, Wyoming, diagnosed a serious heart condition. The prognosis—he might live 5 years or 25 years, depending upon how well he took care. He was immediately discharged from the Air Force.

After working in the insurance field in High Point, North Carolina, and in Memphis, Tennessee, he moved back home to Savannah, Tennessee, and opened Mon-E-Saver in the Rich Building. Like father, like son.

Throwing himself into community activities, H.C. became active in the planning of the annual Catfish Derby. He also coached Little League. His sport was golf which he greatly enjoyed. Proof of his community involvement could regularly be seen in the newspaper. Often H.C. was pictured standing by a future Miss Catfish Derby or with his Little League players.

His enthusiasm was only overshadowed by the knowledge of his weakening heart. Passion for golf increased as his heart decreased in strength. As for his airplane, he had given up his license to fly and sold the airplane.

In 1974 I had an unnerving dream—a dream in which H.C. was depicted as being skin and bones, weak and frail. I prayed until I was exhausted. Finally the tears dried up, and I returned to bed.

The following Saturday with that dream still vivid in my mind, I drove 112 miles to see him. When I arrived in Savannah, he walked out of his store, Mon-E-Saver, and gave me his usual big hug.

After catching up on family news, I introduced the subject of Christ as Savior, but he stated that he did not desire to discuss that topic. With a heavy heart, I dropped the subject. I knew the dream had come from God.

A few months later I was at church on a typical Sunday night. I do not remember the sermon; I do remember the prayer. The Lord touched my heart with these words: "If you don't pray for your brother now, you will never have another opportunity."

This was my brother H.C. about whom God was warning me! This stream was deep, muddy, and murky. I could not see the bottom, but I had to trust the BRIDGE over this gorge.

Even though he had married and left home when I was twelve years old, H.C. had been both a father and a brother to me. When there was a special "suit-wearing" occasion, H.C. had always stood in for Dad. So I prayed—but soon I wondered what should that prayer be? I remembered that in the Bible one person had prayed that his life be extended fifteen years. Finally, I prayed, "Thy perfect will be done."

I remember that in my prayer, I said a word which I had never said before. I had no idea what it meant.

"Eloi. Eloi. lama." These words rolled over and over in my mind.

By this time I was exhausted from intercessory prayer. I discovered I had prayed for an hour and everyone else in the prayer room had left except church staff members.

I knew that my next step would be seeking solitude. I needed to listen to God's directions for that next step.

Then the moment came. I attended a woman's retreat which for four years I had helped to plan, because I was president of the organization. In the midst of the praise—God gave me a personal promise of blessing.

"Betty, anything you ask for right now, you can have."

Without hesitation, I responded, "Lord, I'll take my whole family saved, but I would like to call one by name, my brother H.C."

In May 1976, after an IV was left in H.C.'s arm over three days, he developed a streptococcus infection. H.C. had told the nurse that if she hit a good vein just leave the IV in, as is. Soon he was transferred to intensive care where he battled for his life. Open heart surgery was a last option as doctors declared they could not find another case like his in the medical journals. He was allergic to some of the medicine, and there were complications with others. Doctors had numerous meetings to discuss his medical problems. They finally agreed upon open heart surgery.

The day of surgery, Verlene fasted and I prayed in the chapel for two hours of surgery. As I turned to my Bible, I saw, **"My heart is fixed, O God, my heart is fixed. I will sing and give praise." Psalm 57:7**

This passage comforted me and led me to believe H.C. would survive the surgery.

Dr. Edward Garrett replaced two heart valves and repaired a hole in H.C.'s heart. Surgery did go well, but my brother's body developed two more serious infections. On several occasions the doctor said he didn't think H.C. would make it through the night, but I knew he would. At 135 lbs,. he looked exactly as he had in my dream in 1974.

For weeks, he was in and out of Intensive Care, and his wife Jean spent most nights at the hospital. Meanwhile, one evening, about midnight, I sat down in our den and opened my Bible to Mark 2:3-5 and I read:

And they came unto him, bringing one sick of the palsy, which was borne of four. And when they could not come nigh unto him for the press, they uncovered the roof where he was and when they had broken it up, they let down the bed where the sick of palsy lay. When Jesus saw *their faith*, he saith unto the sick of the palsy, Son, thy sins be forgiven thee.

Two words stood out—"**their faith**."

This man was too ill to walk or to have faith, but God honored the faith of the other four men. They believed that he would be healed if they brought him to the Master. H.C. may be in a semi-comatose state, but if I believe, he will live, I reasoned.

Remembering that my mother had once said, "I can give up a child if I know he is prepared to meet God," I felt my faith increase. I then remembered the verse that I read one night:

"Though our outward man perish, yet the inward man is renewed day by day. " II Corinthians 4:16.

This verse became a reality to me as I saw ways in which God was strengthening H.C.'s spiritual development even as his body grew weaker and weaker.

On one occasion, a minister, Rev. Robert Jones, came to see him in Intensive Care, and H.C. confided to him, "Pastor Jones, do you know what I want you to do today?"

"No, Cubby," was his reply.

"I want you to baptize me."

"Well, that is just what I'll do."

A long pause followed.

"No, on second thought, I want to wait until my whole family can be baptized together," H.C. replied in a weakened raspy voice which resulted from his pulling the tubes out of his throat one day. He had damaged his vocal cords.

Again, he was removed from Intensive Care to a room, and on June 12, 1977, I sat beside him and watched a televised church service during which Drexel's sister-in-law sang a special song.

That evening Jean, H.C's wife, called. In a subdued voice said, "Betty, they say H. C. is dying; if you want to see him alive, you need to come now."

I called my mother and sister in Savannah andthey drove over a hundred miles to the hospital. Jean was crying softly as the hospital chaplain comforted her. Without planning it, I placed my hand on H. C.'s head and quoted these words aloud:

> **"I will lift up mine eyes unto the hills, from whence cometh my help. My help cometh from the Lord, which made heaven and earth. He will not suffer thy foot to be moved; He that keepeth thee will not slumber. "**
> **Psalm 121:1-3**

This passage which I had learned as a teenager had been pulled from my memory bank in order to comfort us or him. I have heard that hearing is the last sense to leave the body.

Two hours later, my mother and sister arrived at the hospital. Hours later on June 13, 1977, H.C, age 51, went to be with His Heavenly Father.

The morning of the funeral I awoke with a heavy heart, with an awful awareness that something was horribly wrong. At first I could not think—in seconds the realization hit me—my H.C. was dead. I would never speak with him again in this life! I would never hear his voice. Deep sadness came over me, but very soon a heavenly joy replaced it. I knew where H.C. was. I had never felt this measure of joy before. It was as though H.C. were telling me, "Betty, why didn't you tell me it was like this? If I had known that heaven was like this, I wouldn't have fought so hard to live."

The words were so clear that I almost responded aloud, "Cubby, I've never been to heaven. I didn't really know."

Then a verse flashed in my mind:

> **"In thy presence is fulness of joy; at thy right hand there are pleasures forevermore." Psalm 16:11**

I had been given a tiny measure of their heavenly happiness.

A few feet from H.C.'s grave is the monument of his great grandfather who served in the Civil War—Alfred Alexander Neill and his wife Sarah Jane "Gabby" Young Neill.

There had been a bridge of love and pride between Cubby and me. The hours of grief covered me like an umbrella as the weeks passed. At times I did not share my umbrella with anyone; instead I folded my grief like a fan and clutched it close to my heart. After a time the memories no longer cut like a sharp blade.

Lovingly, I took out the old photographs and for long periods of time I memorized the image on the paper. The photo of him at age 15—he was a gangly boy with arms and legs that had grown too fast for the rest of his body—thereby giving him the appearance of Ichabod Crane. I smiled at the sight of the two legs that looked like two exclamation points—too skinny for the slouching body—a body with the body mass of a man. It was difficult to tell—was H.C. very laid back or was he totally unconcerned?

Our dear Cubby gave only a faint hint of becoming a comely figure; the drooped shoulders and the short waistline under the long-sleeved white shirt did not really foretell that this casually dressed young man would one day be a politician on the Tennessee Executive Committee for his party and a successful insurance agent.

So is grief—as Camus wrote—it does drop, one drop at a time until its stay becomes so unwelcome it finally fades but never totally disappears.

Questions to Consider:

1. Do you know a moral, mannerly person who needs Jesus? Could you be the one to introduce that person to Him?

2. What has God shown you as you have walked beside a loved one walking through the valley of death?

CHAPTER 13

A Loaf of Bread From Sister Verlene

An incident involving my sister Verlene is a direct confirmation that God not only works in our lives, but he plants his plans for us many years before they materialize.

When Verlene called me on April 27, 1997, she told me what her pastor and a visiting evangelist had shared with her the previous Friday night. After prayer regarding a personal approach to evangelism, her pastor felt in his heart that he should give a gift package to every first time visitor to their church. Furthermore, he had approached my sister with the idea that this gift package should contain a mini loaf of Verlene's sourdough bread. He felt that from this simple act of love a revival would spring forth.

I am always surprised at how God works. I could not wait to pull out my Bible and search for Mark 6:38. There it was! I had written Verlene's name beside this passage on August 11, 1984.

The passage was about the five loaves and two fish and the feeding of the 5,000 men. At the time I read it, I was seated in church and was prompted by the Holy Spirit to think of Verlene's unmistakable talent for baking sourdough bread. Right then I felt that my sister would bake homemade bread and pray over it. Giving it as a gift to church newcomers was even better.

God could use her and this holy loaf to win souls for him. Today, Verlene is called "the Bread Lady" at her church.

In the Bible God always used the ordinary ways to save souls. Being a master of creativity, he asked one man to dip himself in water seven times.

Today he uses the Bread Lady to bring the lost to him. Her "prayed over" bread has reached into many homes and has blessed many tables.

I marvel that my sister has been so molded by her Creator. As I recall our sisterly fights, I recall Verlene's early life, as she no doubt recalls mine. Let me tell you about Verlene. Her stubbornness without a doubt came from the Solomons, and as Mother said on numerous occasions, "You can lead a horse to water, but you can't make it drink." Verlene was that stubborn. As a child, I followed close behind.

Take the time that our father asked Verlene to give up a side of the bed so that I could sleep there. Verlene rolled until she landed on the floor and remained there a long time before moving the width of the bed to sleep beside her sister---ME.

Just as the wind blows and the weather changes, Verlene's facial expressions mirrored the mood that she was in at the time. Her eyes could reflect a mixture of pleasure and pain. Days after she had driven by a wreck on Highway 64 and saw the mutilated body of a young woman, her sleep was restless and filled with dreams of sirens and screeching wheels. Death made a vivid impression upon her tender heart.

Verlene enjoyed excitement and still does. Yet she likes to stay out of the spotlight. She became an accomplished pianist but would never plan the piano in public. My sis who looked a lot like the young Katherine Hepburn, the actress, became a teacher after fifteen years of working in an office. And what a teacher she has been. Children often tell us how she impacted their lives.

That was and is my big sister. Growing up, separated by five years had both its blessing and its curses. I wanted to be as old as she so that I could go to the summer parties where she was a vivacious, animated teenager with an abundance of friends.

Since she was rarely sullen or morose, I guess it was my teasing that brought out her stubbornness. Through it all, there was a cohesive bond between us that could become frayed but would not snap.

Yes, it is with great pleasure that I say I am the sister of Verlene, the Bread Lady.

Questions to Consider:

1. What is the gift that God has given you to use in serving your fellow men and women?

2. Are you using it? If not, how could you take a small step toward using it to serve God?

CHAPTER 14

Two Opposites Make A Life Together

Two opposites married—a perfectionist and a free spirit. I think it was God's will that they should marry; after all, my mother and father were even born in the same house eight years apart.

Although my mother weighed only three pounds at birth, she grew to 5′3″ and inherited the Solomon hands, taking a size eight ring and gloves. She also inherited her seven sneezes and her love of horses from her father. Her enjoyment of travel came from both Mama and Papa Solomon.

As a young child, I soon learned my mother, Zelma Solomon, Rich, exhibited an inner glow of hidden strength. She drew her demarcations and made sure my friends were from good homes because "birds of a feather flock together" and "people will know you by the company you keep"—two of her sayings.

A simple facial expression let me know when I had reached my limit with her patience. Her demeanor could send fear to the bottom of my toes, but on the flip side, I also experienced the depth of her love. Her encouragement could melt my childhood and teenage fears. Yet on occasion her tough love could be too demanding.

But Mother's heart had a bent toward God, and our religious training came from her. "Be sure your name is written in the Lamb's Book of Life. Betty, the most important thing is to know you are going to heaven." This was her frequent refrain for her children and grandchildren. Her grandchildren would laughingly repeat the well-known phrase back to her at all family gatherings. They were well aware of grandmother's desire for each of them.

She had her opposite---her husband, my father.

Fishing reminded me of my Dad. Every April, my father with his well-tanned face would set his alarm clock for 4:00 a.m. He was going fishing. In April the striped bass were biting.

Each day before he would open the restaurant and serve breakfast to customers--mostly fishermen who came to Pickwick-- he had already caught a string of fish. Fishermen were aware that he knew what he was talking about when he discussed fishing. They also wanted to buy his artificial lures.

Likewise, everything about baseball, my father remembered. He quoted player's averages and knew every World Series winner for years back. I was aware that the one regret of his life was not getting to play with the Brooklyn Dodgers. When they asked him to sign a contract, he chose to stay in Savannah with his family. At that time, the salary offered to players was meager; Dad made his choice, but it was still hard for him to see his friend, Hank Deberry, sign a contract for a professional team. Baseball was the love of his youth.

I liked to go turkey and squirrel hunting with my Dad. I went with him when I was so young he had to lift me over the briers, the blackberry bushes and thorns. He always had a turkey caller or a gobbler, as I called it. There were two pieces of cedar attached at one end. Then there was a corncob on a stem which he would rub across this piece of wood and make it gobble like a turkey. One of the best at this, he could fool any turkey that came along.

No man ever loved children like he did. His patience with me was unending. Consequently, I grew up thinking that every father was just like him.

Questions to Consider:

1. Can you see that the traits God gave your parents have in turn been beneficial when exhibited in you today?
2. Who is your role model today?

CHAPTER 15

Moving On Up—Mother and Daddy Join H.C.

At the end of his life, in fact, as I sat before his casket, I could hear the other fishermen asking Dad, "Clyde, what's biting?" "Where are you fishing today?" "Near the boils?" "Did you use artificial or live bait?"

Oh, how he loved me. I knew he loved children—others saw it too. After we were married, Drexel called to my attention how much Dad loved children. As a result, I never had difficulty believing that God was a Heavenly Father who loved me more than I could comprehend.

H.C., Verlene, and I took traits from both parents, but certainly our extraordinary love for children came from our father. Children touch heartstrings. Dad's way with children influenced Verlene to devote thirty years to teaching and caused me to devote my entire professional life to working with children of all ages. I understood how they thought and how they felt. I could communicate with the youngest—age two, three, or four—it did not matter. There was a rapport there that was treasured. Children are indeed a gift from God.

In 1966, eights years before my father's death, he suffered a massive stroke which paralyzed his left side. Any questions I asked him he answered correctly, but he never again initiated a conversation.

I was teaching school at Wooddale High when the call came from my husband—the call stating that Dad had a problem.

"Drexel, he's dead, isn't he?"

"Yes, he is."

That October 1974, very early in the morning hours, I remember praying, "If there's anything that I am to do at Dad's funeral, Lord, bring it to my mind."

This thought came. Get a small white Bible and give it to Verlene to place in Dad's paralyzed hand the last time the casket is opened.

My sister and Dad had a unique relationship. She and I made a joke of it and said, "Well, if you want anything from Dad, send Verlene to ask for it."

The Bible I found had a picture of the Prodigal Son returning to his father. I knew that was the Bible Dad should have, for after he was bedridden, this formerly very busy businessman and sportsman had listened to the Holy Spirit. He had told Verlene he wanted to be baptized.

Regretting his delay, I wished he had made his decision earlier and might have avoided some family conflicts. For me, family life was never the same again after visitations had to be separately. God's perfect will needs to be our goal.

On the day of his funeral, Verlene placed the Bible in Dad's hand. In eternity, I will know how many people were moved by that gesture. I believe all of us were.

On May 3, 1999, my mother became the bride of Christ. Words I had memorized in 1984 came to mind:

> **"Let us be glad and rejoice, and give honor to him, for the marriage of the Lamb is come, and his wife hath made herself ready. And to her was granted that she should be arrayed in fine linen, clean and white: for the fine linen is the righteousness of saints. And he saith to me, Blessed are they which are called unto the marriage supper of the Lamb." Revelation 19**

In the weeks leading to Mother's going home to be with the Lord, I prayed for my visit to fall when she would be alert. Then I prayed that I could do something for her. One thing I discovered, the Lord is aware of each situation and has a specific plan for the elderly at this particular time in their lives. He has made that promise to them:

> **"...I am the Lord, thy God, which teacheth thee to profit, which leadeth thee by the way that thou shouldest go." Isaiah 48:17**

As the saying goes, "We see the back of the quilt top with its threads and knots, but the Lord sees the top side only and that side is perfect."

Even the fact that Mother had broken her hip while at church was filtered through God's hands. This, too, God had allowed, and it became a part of his plan for her life. **"For I know the thoughts that I think toward you," saith the Lord, "thoughts of peace, and not of evil." Jeremiah 29:11**

Mother had instilled two things in me—a love for learning and knowledge and a love of God, while my father gave me a love of reading, children, animals and sports. Mother told me over and over again, "The most important thing a girl can do for herself is get a good education."

I believed her. My dream was synonymous with hers. It was difficult to see her confined to a hospital bed in Patterson Woods across the street from my childhood home. Even though the house has been replaced with a lumber company and a bank, we are still in there somewhere because our childhood voices still ring as I drive by.

Several years before this day, I had been studying a Bible Study while riding with Drexel from Memphis to Savannah. As I studied, the idea came to me to get someone to sew a banner with my mother's favorite verse on it. Immediately, I shared the idea with my husband, and surprisingly two days later we saw a banner hanging over a choir at church: P.U.S.H.: Pray Until Something Happens. An announcement explained that our church secretary had been responsible for ordering the banner. Drexel looked at me and said, "Find out where she ordered it."

I did. One week later, I ordered the banner with Mother's favorite verse: **Psalm 150:6—"Let everything that hath breath praise the Lord. Praise ye the Lord."**

That week when I talked by phone with Barry in Florida, his immediate reaction to our newly purchased banner was, "Why don't you hang it in her room at the nursing home in order to be a permanent witness?"

Drexel took his drill and the banner to the nursing home. This banner, in gold and purple, colors of royalty, heralded Psalm 150:6 to every nurse, doctor, aide, visitor, or maintenance person who entered Mother's room. We were grateful to the administration for allowing us to hang the banner to proclaim Mother's faith in a living God.

Mother couldn't do much speaking for herself; however, she still had her lucid times. One that I recall came at 4:00 a.m. when our phone rang in our son's Florida home. Numb all over, fearful of who might be calling, I stumbled to the phone. Even now I stand amazed at the images that passed through my mind between the bed and the phone: a well, a diaper, a garden, a smokehouse, a rooster, a yard, a house, a family of five, a fireplace, a night before Christmas and death—to name a few. Finally, I took the phone from my son's hand.

My astonished sister at the Hardin County Nursing Home explained that she was putting our 90-year-old Mother on the line. Mother had begun to speak in sentences, and Verlene had been notified by the nursing home personnel.

What a blessed serendipity to hear my mother's voice a thousand miles away in Savannah, Tennessee. Her words were a treasured drink of cold spring water. I stored each sentence, a wealth of memories and love for the future.

We told family stories about happy-go-lucky children and Clyde and Zelma supplying all their needs. I told Mother I was recording family events. I asked her if she wanted me to take her riding so she could see downtown Savannah. She eagerly answered with "Yes."

This phone call was indeed a blessing from above. God had answered my prayers that Mother would know us until the end of life. When I heard her say, "Verlene., " I remembered that my sister had prayed especially that Mother would be able to call her by name.

> **"...Great and marvelous are thy works, Lord, God Almighty..." Revelation 15:3**

Now off the phone, I continued to think of stories of my times with Mother. I thought about the vacation to North Carolina and Gatlinburg in 1985. In our motel room I slept soundly until I awoke with a start. I concluded there must be an urgency to pray for God's protection. I asked Him, "What do you want me to pray for?"

His response was unmistakably, " For your safety."

I prayed for safety for the next morning, shared this message from God with my mother and sister, then, in faith, we traveled to North Carolina.

After stopping for lunch, we came upon a terrible wreck at the bottom of a long incline. A double-wide trailer was now a splintered pile of lumber and twisted metal. Wrecked cars were strewn all along the side of the road.

My mother said, "Now I see the reason why you prayed for protection last night. Had we left sooner, our car would be one of those along the roadside!"

In talking with doctors after the 4:00 a.m. phone call from Mother, we learned the prognosis was that Mother would die soon after this last goodbye. Not so. I returned to Savannah to see her. As she slept, I looked out the windows at the stately oaks in Patterson Woods, trees near our childhood home place, branches stretching forth in a myriad of directions motionless against the cloudless blue sky. And Mother rested in her bed nearby.

Even though her blood sugar had spiked to an alarming 900, there were welcome sounds of her breathing. Here I was across the street from where I was at age three, and one mile from where I was at age eleven, and two blocks from Mother's present white brick house. All of my childhood memories were formed and my character shaped within one mile of the Hardin County Courthouse and Savannah's landing on the Tennessee River. Quietly sitting here, I focused on that tight circle of my life.

I decided maybe that is the reason I have such a strong attachment to water—the water that surrounds this hometown—lakes, creeks, rivers. I am always at peace near water, even that of the ocean. As a child I would ride with my father in a small boat on the Tennessee River to check the trout lines or with H.C. as we water skied at Pickwick Lake. As I reminisced, I concluded that God knew what He was doing when he created water and placed me near it.

The Apostle John saw **"a pure river of water of life"** flowing from **"the throne of God and of the Lamb." Revelation 22:1** Then in Verse 17, he says, "**And whosoever will, let him take the water of life freely."** God leaves it all to us as a matter of free will. God does not want a puppet on a string. He relishes our choice to come to Him.

Barry flew home from Florida to see Grandmother Rich on Saturday, and in a weak, raspy voice she said, "I knew you'd come." The next night, Mother went home to be with the Lord.

Many thoughts coursed through my mind as I heard the familiar verses of "Holy Ground." Then it was my turn to give the eulogy. I walked up to the front of the chapel with Mother's grandsons, Barry and Randy, to follow me with their remembrances. All I could think as I approached the podium was "I must not cry. I want to do this for Mother." Following my eulogy Randy and Barry shared their treasured memories of Grandmother Rich.

As we left the grave, I thought of the importance of one life. Many say, "I am but one person. What effect can I have on this world?" I can say that this one life—my mother's life had a great effect on all of the people she met. Her calling was a one-on-one testimony and ministry.

God used her because she was a willing vessel.

Questions to Consider:

1. When a parent dies, how is a child's world changed spiritually?

2. Do you see yourself as one who is engaged to Christ or who will someday be His bride? If not, what would you need to do to be His bride?

3. Do you see that you do not have to be perfect to be used by God?

CHAPTER 16

Elease Teachers Her Niece By Example

Like most people of my generation, I heard adult conversation about extended family members. Evening meal conversations sometimes centered around what will we do if Dad breaks his hip? Or, why is Verlene choosing this or that option? Or, H.C. must learn to take care of himself.

Those conversations even reached beyond the inner family circle to include aunts and uncles. At times I have wondered if aunts and uncles were not added to the family simply to be used as examples to teach children how to live.

Sunday afternoons became family gathering day, and in my childhood, first one relative, then another walked through our house and passed the time of day. During those "passages" I—with my big ears—took in much information that has greatly influenced me to this day. Through it all, I have concluded: One should never discount the influence of a family member on a child.

Certainly my mother's sister Elease made a lasting impression upon my life.

As a child, I thought Elease was a perfect person. As the years went by, I began to see that she liked to control. Her technique to gain control had been cultivated during her childhood years. A beautiful child with striking auburn hair, Elease planned to subvert her older sister; however, spunky Zelma challenged her maneuvers.

All of this give and take characterized their relationship, but the bond of love between them held fast and secure. In fact, Zelma named her oldest daughter for Elease by giving her the name of Mabel Verlene—Elease's name was Mabel Elease.

At times, misery clung to Elease like static electricity. Reacting to some problems in the early years of their marriage, she told her husband that she would never forgive him. Her goal, at times, seemed to be "making him pay" as she wore her tightly wrapped afghan of resentment.

Work became the salvation of the marriage of Elease and Hobert. They purchased land and built a motel at River Heights. Hobert kept the grounds mowed, the flowers planted and weeded, and the swimming pool clean. Oddly, the results of their hard work appeared to give them the glue they needed for fulfillment and degrees of happiness.

True happiness came from being with their grandson Billy Jack who was the light and joy of their lives. I shall always remember Hobert's passion for Arby's roast beef sandwiches.

One day as Elease cooked and served food in the restaurant, I heard her say, "I would rather clean house than cook." No doubt that was true for all relatives and friends knew Elease kept a meticulously clean house.

She had an explanation for her cleaning—"It works off my nervousness."

In later years, Elease and Hobert sold the motel and moved to Ft. Myers, Florida, where they first lived at 11A Bayside before they moved to the gated community in Jamaica Bay at 24 Galenta Court. Here Elease engaged in shuffleboard contests where she won numerous trophies. As her niece, I had many precious memories of traveling with Elease and Hobert from Tennessee to Miami, to Key West, to Pompano and to Ft. Myers, and, of course, memories of enjoying her delicious Christmas dinners ending with orange cake and chocolate pie.

Later they moved closer to Ft. Myers Beach in the Thunderbird Court on Rosa Lee Street before buying and remolding the house at 12 Derwent. Elease had her mother's knack for buying and selling homes.

We loved her in spite of her stubborn will because she was our relative. She didn't have to be perfect. She was "family."

At the time Elease was living in the house at 12 Derwent, I had a dream about her and Hobert. Eight words of the dream appeared to be prophetic.

Drexel and I were sleeping in one of Mother's guest rooms while Hobert and Elease occupied the second guest room with the twin beds that Elease had sold to Mother when she and Hobert had moved from Savannah to Ft. Myers. Mother, wanting to provide a nice place for her sister to stay when she and Hobert came to visit each summer, in turn sold her antique bedroom suite to make way for the twin beds. As a result, Elease and Hobert drove from Ft. Myers and spent three months with Mother each summer.

In my dream, as I slept in the bedroom next to theirs, I saw their only child, Hobert, Jr. tears running down his face, kneeling before God. As he prayed, I heard the words, "Thou shalt be saved and thy whole family." I marveled at the powerful, majestic voice and buried the words in my heart. As I pondered their meaning, I could hear the squeak of Mother's porch swing. Then I heard the voices of Mother and Elease as they were having their early morning coffee on the porch.

Grabbing my housecoat, combing my hair, and washing my face, I hurried to join them on the porch with my preferred cup of spiced tea.

As I entered the kitchen, Hobert was standing by the coffee maker pouring a cup of coffee. Here was a man I had known all my life, one who had helped to build the Arch Bridge over the Indian Creek at Olive Hill in 1924. One who had been in and out of our home for years—time had passed and now he was 80-years-old.

Feeling a prompting by the Holy Spirit, I told him, "I had a unique dream last night." Then I plunged ahead, "Would you mind if I shared it with you, Uncle Hobert?"

"Sure, go ahead."

"I dreamed that I saw Hobert, Jr. kneeling with tears streaming down his face. Then I heard these words, words spoken with great authority: "Thou shalt be saved and thy whole family."

There we stood, as we broached a subject which seemed difficult simply because we knew each other so well.

I saw a man who had worked his life away—worked hours beyond the necessary 40-hour week to cover for the misery of marital problems that occurred in their early marriage. Tears flowed down his weathered face, for Hobert had mellowed as he had worked in his flower beds and manicured his lawn. On numerous occasions he had begged his wife for forgiveness, but she continued to refuse.

He responded, "I hope you're right, Betty. I hope you're right. Hobert, Jr. doesn't obey his heart specialist who wants him to stop smoking cigarettes."

"Hobert, this wasn't just an ordinary dream. It was more. It was a dream from God."

He quietly wept and our conversation ended.

Over one year later, I felt compelled to share this dream with his son (my first cousin) Hobert, Jr. The phone rang, and it was my cousin calling from his home in Olive Branch, Mississippi. As the conversation progressed, the door was open for me to share the dream.

Silence.

Then with a voice choked with emotion, he whispered, "Sis, I have been going to Central Church, and I really like it."

God had opened the door. He had nudged me, and I had stepped through. Now I was released from the knowledge that God had shared a promise with me, which I was obliged to pass on to Hobert and his son. Because of the love we had for each other, I wanted him to spend eternity with me. He was the only cousin who had lived with my family for a year at Patterson Place. Family ties are strong. At the time of the dream, I did not know that in six years the entire Beckham family would have passed on.

I did not know that Uncle Hobert would be taken by multiple tumors of the brain. Life continued to be rearranged. Two years later Elease was diagnosed with lung cancer, and Mother fell in the church parking lot when a young man accidentally knocked her down. After two surgeries, a ball and socket, followed by hip replacement, Mother was then transferred to a nursing home where she could receive physical therapy.

After Mother wasn't living at home, we invited Elease to come to Mother's house in Savannah for her three-month summer visit. After driving from Florida, she went to the specialist in Jackson, Tennessee, in order to check out a persistent cough. Elease, a nonsmoker, had lung cancer. That summer she received treatments, wore a wig and lived as a widow alone in Mother's house with Zelma in the nursing home, only three blocks away, and their youngest sister Maude also nearby.

On August 15, 1993, we gave Elease the only birthday party of her life. Mother's house was crowded with relatives both in and out of town. Later that week Elease called me to her bedside…she was in great pain. She asked me to pray for her.

We had a sweet prayer together.

Dear God,

Cover Aunt Elease with your feathers (Psalm 91:4) Keep her under your wings as she trusts you daily. May your

Truth be her shield and buckler. Please help her to sleep free from pain.

Amen.

Later that month a very weak 80-year-old Elease drove by herself about 1000 miles to Ft. Myers to see her home for the last time. The strong "Solomon will" intact, she was able to stay in her own house for a few weeks. Then, when her pain grew unbearable, she summoned her grandson Billy Jack of Olive Branch, Mississippi, to bring her to Memphis where she entered Cordova Healthcare Facility.

On December 7, 1993, she said her last words to me:

"What do you want for Christmas?" I asked during an afternoon visit.

"I won't be here," was her reply.

Knowing her strong will and not sure what she meant, I asked, "Where will you be?"

"In heaven."

The next day when I drove from Memphis to Savannah to see Mother, I took along a black dress, suitable for a funeral service. I knew in my heart I had visited Elease for the last time.

Two days later her voice was stilled by God. I wore the black dress as I listened to my first cousin, Rev. Larry Paul Rich, preside at her funeral. The reality of Acts 16: 31 came alive to me: **"Believe on the Lord Jesus Christ, and Thou shalt be saved, and thy house."**

To celebrate Elease's homegoing were Hobert, Jr., Billy Jack, Verlene, Larry Paul, Mother's and Elease's nephew, and his two sisters, Faye and Linda, who were the children of Maude, who had married my father's cousin, Duel Rich. Larry, Faye and Linda—as children—had sung for the Catfish Derby, the local radio station, WORM, and had auditioned for the Ted Mack Show.

This family circle stood by Elease's grave and visualized all of the trophies that she had so proudly won in her shuffle-boarding. Trophies—but of no eternal value! All of that effort and of no value now! My thoughts returned to the verse: **"Put up your treasures in heaven where nothing can corrupt them and where no burglar can break in and steal." Matthew 6:20** (NIV)

Elease was with her earthly father and with her heavenly Father, and I was left behind treasuring the memories of the good times.

Jealousy had separated sisters Elease and Zelma at times when they were young, but love had built a bridge to save their relationship. Upon hearing her sister had gone on to be with the Lord, Mother's 88-year-old weakened voice quietly cried, "Oh, Elease, Elease!" On numerous occasions thereafter Mother was heard calling out in great sorrow her sister's name.

Beside the grave, our priorities of times passed played out. I was so happy to recall every moment I had shared with this aunt. Times when my own responsibilities had made the effort to be with Elease difficult—so happy was I now that I had shoved aside the agenda and had driven Elease to Memphis when Hobert had been diagnosed with the multiple tumors in his brain. I was so thankful I had been in Ft. Myers at that time to help my aunt. I knew my availability had been God's planning.

Also, at the grave I sadly recalled Elease's words to her best friend, "I should have told Hobert that I forgave him before he died." Her pride had caused her to wait too long before making peace. Bitterness is an evil bedfellow; peace of mind is to be cherished.

At the graveside we see the urgency involved in relationships. The "before it's too late" is played out beside the red clay of the cemetery more vividly than at any other time.

At the time of my dream I did not know that cancer of the brain would take my Uncle Hobert from us in 1991; the lung cancer would also claim Aunt Elease in 1993; and heart disease and crippling arthritis would snatch 65-year-old Hobert, Jr. in 1997.

That reaper, Death, had taken the entire Beckham family of three within six years of the dream. That prophetic dream comforted me at the funerals of each member of the Beckham family. Further comfort--the memory of Elease's last words to me on December 7, 1993, were buried in cement: "In heaven."

Questions to Consider:

1. Consider how a nonbeliever has made a lasting impression upon your life?

2. How could you have the joy of seeing that person come to Jesus Christ?

3. Do you know someone upon whom misery clings like static electricity? How can that bondage be broken from the life of such a believer?

4. Is there somebody that we need to forgive? Why is forgiveness so hard? Is it because of pride?

BRIDGING THIS WORLD AND THE NEXT... HOMEGOING

What unfinished business do I need to transact with the one who is passing on?

Forgiveness

Assurance of medical care to the end

Expressions of Love

Assurance of taking care of business

Expressions of Appreciation

Assurance it is okay to go on to their reward

What kind of care will my loved one need?

Do I have fences to mend?

Does my loved one have "peace like a river glorious"?

Have I arranged for final prayers, communion, or baptism for them?

Have they met with those they have mentored along the way?

Have I learned what is important and what is not important in the house?

Have the final blessings been passed on?

Have I considered how I will memorialize the special gifts of this loved one?

Do I see a picture of the enlarging heavenly circle as my loved one passes on?

Does my loved one have a problem with parting with earthly possessions?

Has my loved one had the opportunity to see people and places for the final time?

What are the verses, poems, passages that reflect my loved one's life?

How can I guard, as much as possible, the indignity of wasting away?

Do I remember that it was not in God's original plan that we should taste of death…therefore there is rarely death with dignity?

Bridging The Years That Foster Trouble

CHAPTER 17

The Speed Bump Years

In the year of general unrest and the ultimate Memphis City School teacher strike of 1978, I served as principal of Whitehaven Elementary--a school without a full staff of teachers! As a result, parents volunteered and classes were combined. All of my life I had heard that trouble comes in bunches, and I was about to see my own bunches of trouble very close to home.

With this 1978 vigilance at school, I found outside-of-school appointments too much for my schedule. However, I did successfully work in a routine eye exam. During that appointment, the optometrist discovered a problem that he wanted a specialist to examine—his diagnosis was that I had torn retinas in both eyes. Immediate surgery followed for the left eye in September, the right eye in October.

On the morning of the first surgery, I read Isaiah 52:12 in The Living Bible: **"For the Lord will go ahead of you, and he, the God of Israel, will protect you from behind."**

Like any double, follow-up surgery, I dreaded the second one in October, for I now knew the pain and dreaded the restraint of having my hands tied to my sides before taking the anesthetic. Yet, at the same time that I recalled the pain, I knew that I would have the surgery. I didn't want to be blind.

From her Savannah home, Mother came to be with me for the second surgery. Her prayers were a comfort for me. I memorized a verse from the Living Bible to carry with me into the cold surgical suite: Psalm 112: 6: **"Such a man will not be overthrown by evil circumstances. God's constant care of him will make a deep impression on all who see it."** I was not afraid as the hospital personnel honored my request that they tie my hands after they had administered the anesthetic.

The following week, I returned to my turbulent place of school administrator. Two restrictions confined me: Do not bend over.

Do not lift an object weighing over 10 lbs. To add insult to injury—as the old timers used to say—I wore a patch over my right eye, and my left eye was dilated with eye drops. Thankfully, I had inherited the fighting spirit of Papa Os, since not being able to see to read is a major handicap for a school principal.

School challenges did not go away just because I was recovering from surgery. As I looked at our circumstances, I was once again reminded of my belief that education and religion are the twin towers of civilization. Once again, I had seen education as the strong fort and religion as the force against brutality.

Our 530 school students had a strong need to believe in something and to belong to a group. If they didn't believe in God, they would believe in another force. Prayer, by mandate of the Supreme Court, had been taken from the schools; therefore, all we had left was a time of silence before the school day began. Prayers outside school--at home were all that could plead for God to bring to pass His will in these young people's lives. I knew I was leading by example. I also realized that a wise teacher makes learning a joy. To deal with discipline problems, I prayed for wisdom.

As in most experiences there is a flip side. In this school of somewhat unfriendly unrest were wholesome, interested students that I also led. Many positive improvements were instituted that year. We were adopted by two industries—Tension Envelope and the Army Depot. We initiated Grandparent's Day. I asked a college coach's wife, Mrs. Larry Finch, to train a group of cheerleaders since her children attended my school and her husband was on my Principal's Advisory Board. Together with the teachers and parents, we raised funds to air-condition the library and to expand the activities of field day.

Four years into my "speed bump" years, I continued to faithfully take the bridge provided for me—Jesus Christ—when on February 10, 1982, my mother-in-law, after suffering for eight months, died of cancer. Because of her extended illness, we traveled to be with her as much as possible; therefore, I delayed my own, yet another surgery, until June 21, 1982. We closed school for the summer, completed the annual audit, and began the summer with surgery. To prepare for this operation, I prayed and was comforted by Psalm 128: 2: **"Happy shalt thou be, and it shall be well with thee."**

Like anyone, I was happy to have this surgery behind me, but I did have peace as I was transported into the surgical corridor;

still I wondered what additional trials awaited me. This period of my life---this time of one physical problem after another, had lasted much longer than I would ever have imagined in my younger years. Sometimes these speed bumps can magnify themselves in our minds until they appear to be mountains.

I noted that a part of the bridge that God has provided is Intercessory Prayer. We were never intended to carry burdens alone. We must ask for prayer and not be so proud that we do not share the load of our burdens with others. (Romans 8: 26-27.) Other verses from my Bible helped me:

Romans 8:34: "Who is he that condemneth? It is Christ that died, yea, rather, that is risen again, who is even at the right hand of God, who also maketh intercession for us."

Hebrews 7: 25: "Wherefore he is able also to save them to the uttermost that come unto God by him, seeing he ever liveth to make intercession for them."

Summer break started in June of 1984; again, I had to schedule surgery. In the spring as I was treated for allergies, my physician saw a nodule on my thyroid that "needed watching." I didn't want to watch it. I wanted it removed altogether.

On the morning of this surgery, preceding my operation was the surgery of another patient revealing a throat malignancy. I gave thanks to my Creator as I lay in my bed in Baptist Hospital—my own nodule had tested negative.

Indeed the Lord was keeping me as I went through difficult times. I was keenly aware of the bridge in my life—the bridge that carried me from illness to health. I tightly gripped the railing on the side of my hospital bed, for I needed His security as I crossed this "bunches of trouble" stream.

Looking back over this valley of sorrow, coupled with work difficulties, I see a principle for anyone who travels this road of the Christian life: Take the bridge and do not wander in the valley looking for an alternate route. The currents in the rivulet under the bridge can be swift and dangerous. The valley can harbor deadly snakes and wild animals. The bridge is much safer and more secure. Jesus is a strong tower; in Him we have an anchor.

Some summers (for the teachers and the students); some Christmas seasons (for all); some birthdays when we are traditionally honored—some traditionally happy times in our lives will be overshadowed with great disappointment and perhaps, sorrow. For a full decade I went from being forewarned of my brother's death to the summer of my fourth major surgery—with all that transpired in between. From that decade I learned the following:

1. Have a relationship with God in place before you reach this time in your life. Know the joy of prayer before you come to the day of calling on him in an hour of desperation.
2. Be prepared to recall Scriptures, passages which mean much to you.
3. Remember: The Christian goes through most of the same things that the nonbeliever experiences. The difference—God goes with the believer, the nonbeliever goes alone.
4. Often, as with me, the experience leads the suffering one to see a clear directive from God--on June 27, 1982, I knew I was to write a book.

Also, I found that I could go through the most difficult times and enjoy the most fruitful times of my professional life simultaneously.

Parallel to my work, during the speed bump years, was that of Drexel. In 1975, he had been named chief of his department and had served as president of AART and had received the Wise Owl Award from the American Association of Rehabilitative Therapy. Then in the year when I had the two eye surgeries, he encouraged me and, at the same time, was promoted at work. In 1983 Governor Lamar Alexander presented Drexel with the Governor's Outstanding Tennessean Award, related to the service he rendered while serving on the Governor's Committee on Employment of the Handicapped. During that same period he served on the Easter Seal Board, with the Lion's Club and the Gideons.

I recall these activities and awards to illustrate how, with God walking beside him through his wife's four rather serious surgeries, Drexel was able to go through it all victoriously. At the same time he made these strides at work and in the community, he was serving the Lord, his community, and caring for me—principal of Whitehaven Elementary School on Elvis Presley Blvd.

Through it all, we endured. That is what happens when we have the bridge—Jesus, with us, for it would be impossible to accomplish all of this without the supernatural help of our Savior.

In 1984 when my health was returning to normal, I became principal of Manor Lake Elementary with an African American student body of 625, K-6. Previously, I had been recruited to be principal at Fox Meadow's Elementary, a school only fifteen minutes from my house with a racially mixed student body.

To make the decision of where to go, I prayed. My answer to prayer came and was confirmed when I walked through the door of Manor Lake. A feeling of peace came over me, and I knew this was where I was to be principal in 1984.

This school was open-concept with my office in the middle of the large multiple classroom building. From my desk I could see all of the students from grades two through four. I became a Career Ladder III principal that year because of a wonderful group of students—95% attendance—and a great faculty and staff. The governor of Tennessee had initiated the selection process. There were tests, evaluations by students, teachers, and superiors, along with observations by out-of-state peers.

As I completed much of the paperwork required for this selection process, the entire world of education was shaken to the core.

On January 28, 1986, I was in the audio-visual room with some upper classmen when the spaceship Challenger was launched. For weeks everyone in the field of education had been elated because a fellow teacher was on that space ship—the first teacher to ride into space. However, only seconds after lift-off, a shocked silence filled the room. The Challenger had exploded before our eyes. It took several minutes for us to process what we had just seen. Everyone aboard that space ship had died in a fiery explosion.

In the days to come we watched multiple replays on television of this tragic event. We later learned there had been a flaw in the design of the solid rocket booster. Empathizing with the families, we regretted that educator, wife, and mother, Christa McCullough, so full of life and courage had died attempting to be the first teacher in space.

Every student knew a teacher. Some had been acquainted with death in their families, but many had not. Now they had seen death face to face. Those days were full of anguish.

Immediately after the explosion of The Challenger, the final word came that I had achieved the status of Career Ladder III Principal, an award given to educators in the state of Tennessee. I credit this achievement to God, to the faculty and staff, to my peers, and to the student body. I loved the children and had a true sense of belonging to Manor Lake. The children were a part of me and the glue to keep me seeking the bridge during these speed bump years.

Accepting the accomplishment and, with the children, mourning the loss of the dream of Christa McCullough, I recalled a day, June 9, 1985, when I was studying the Book of Revelation. In my notes that day, I wrote that this book, to the sinner, is all about the beast, devil, demons, lake of fire, plagues, and the mark of the beast. To the Christian, however, the book of Revelation is about peace, happiness, eternal life, blessing, glory, honor, power, and great, marvelous works. The purpose of Revelation is to magnify Jesus Christ. For the Christian, the book promises a blessing. **"Blessed is he that readeth and they that hear the words of this prophecy, and keep those things which are written therein: for the time is at hand." Revelation 1:3**

At that time I felt God spoke to my heart. Just as He had spoken to John, using his first name throughout the book of Revelation, God had placed in my heart the task of teaching this study at my church, because each time I studied these twenty-two chapters of the final book of the Bible, five hours seemed like two. Food was unimportant. I learned John had been instructed, by God, to write what he had seen; I also felt I had been instructed, by God, to teach a class on this book.

Obediently, I taught a Bible Study for women at my church. Three weeks after teaching the class in 1996, I scheduled a seminar at Pickwick, Tennessee, to speak near my hometown. Music would be provided by Verlene Stanfield, Becky Sibley, and Peggy Lee Lasley. I asked Barbara Kolwyck of Waverly, Tennessee, to act the part of John and to tell us what he saw in the first chapter of the book. After she had finished and after Nell Hawkins had read a short passage in the Bible, I was prepared to share a synopsis of Revelation.

God had other plans.

After I arrived at Pickwick and had dinner with twenty people, I became violently ill. I went straight to the motel room while my husband prepared the room for our early morning session. By midnight, I agreed to go to the hospital. After checking into the hospital and having x-rays, I insisted that Drexel, with assistance from his sister, Wanda Kirkman, return to Pickwick and handle the next day's conference. He was able to set up a video camera to tape what I was missing. Before he left the hospital, he insisted that the tests be taken to be certain I did not have appendicitis. The doctor assured him that I had a virus.

Extremely weak with a high white blood count and low blood pressure, I did not feel like talking or opening my eyes. Yet I knew there were forty Christians praying for me at Pickwick. I trusted their prayers and my God as the IV fluid began to run through my veins.

On Monday morning after the conference weekend had ended, I was released from the local hospital and rode the two hours to Memphis, my eyes closed, extremely ill and wincing with pain the entire trip. Oddly, six months earlier I had scheduled my yearly physical exam for 1:00 p.m. on that day. We took the appointment.

When the doctor saw the x-rays, he immediately sent me to Baptist Hospital and scheduled a surgeon to perform one more test. At 8:00 p.m., I had surgery for a ruptured appendix.

As I look back on that chain of events, I see how God had his hand on my life, and how he had guarded my life by placing me in a position where I had forty Christians praying for me. Six months before I needed the doctor's appointment, I made it for the exact hour when my life was in extreme danger.

Once again, in my "bunches of trouble," God had guarded my life. The steel in the bridge easily transported me across this abyss.

Questions to Consider:

1. Have you a support system to incorporate into your own life as you face surgery or frightening medical tests?

2. When trouble in your own life "came in bunches," did the whole scenario build faith or did it move you far away from Jesus Christ?

3. If so, how can you draw near to Him now?

CHAPTER 18

The Flood In The House

Trials appear to come to us in waves. In my own life there was the 1975-1985 wave and then in 1989 another wave of a different type rushed in.

First I had taught students in high school and in college; then I built bridges for them by opening doors of primary colors—red, green, blue, and yellow---and by serving for eleven years as an elementary principal. Next came the time to retire from the thirty years as an educator, no more training and seminars—"Personal Dynamics," "Principles of Dynamic Leadership," "Leadership Styles," "Time Management," "Stress Management," and "Adopt-a-School" conferences. The whole country had been my work area—Los Angles, Washington, D.C., New Orleans, Detroit, Atlanta, Orlando, Miami and initially Nashville. Much time had been invested in my training and skills.

How would God choose to use me now?

Once the retirement was complete, Drexel and I headed to Florida for our 18th Christmas season in the sun. We enjoyed Christmas with Barry and then returned home the first week in January to weather that was extremely cold.

As we stood at our back door, Drexel found the right door key at the same time I heard what I thought was running water.

"Drexel, I hear running water.! Something is wrong!"

Alarmed we hurriedly opened the door to be greeted by three to four inches of standing water all over the main floor of the house.

"Betty, wait. You can't go inside. I'll get my old rubber boots out of the storage room."

But first he ran to turn off the main water valve at the street. Soon we began our tour of our familiar rooms. The ceiling from the second floor had caved in under the weight of water-saturated insulation and had fallen onto the furniture below. Couches and chairs were ruined, pictures soaked, and carpet saturated. And to add to our wounded spirits, the walls had even mildewed in the two weeks we were enjoying the Florida sun.

What could have caused this mess? The answer was one pinhead hole in a copper pipe leading from the attic to the icemaker. Confusion abounded in mind and spirit as we contacted our insurance agent and booked a Holiday Inn for the remainder of the week. Memphis had been hit with a rare December hard freeze which had frozen water pipes here and in other homes.

To make matters worse for us, in the last months before my retirement, we had carefully put the house in mint condition for the years when our income would be retirement funds only. Room by room we had done a few touches of redecorating, chosen a few pieces of special furniture we had always wanted. Like any other couple, we surmised we should make these changes now, for later we might feel we couldn't afford to do so. The house, yard, automobiles were made ready for this big change in our lives.

I was numb. For a few hours, I didn't know where to begin. Finally, I decided the furniture could be replaced; I must salvage the family pictures—a baby step I had taken into a task that would take weeks and weeks before completion.

For the next four months we lived in the Club Corporate apartment on Germantown Parkway; I named this period of our lives—the Flood.

To make the whole situation more inconvenient, Drexel had not yet put in his final days at work. I was the one who had retired. As he went to work each day, I slogged through the awesome task of listing and pricing each item from shoes to stove to curtains to carpets to tables to thawed frozen foods.

One day, very cold and weary from my inventory taking, I finally sat down to count the real cost of this devastation. A feeling of sadness came over me; I felt as if I had suffered the loss of a dear family member. Day after day as the temperature in Memphis remained unseasonably low, my spirits reciprocated. The bare concrete floors chilled my feet as I walked through each day to view the work in progress. Soon I realized others had endured this same "bad scene" and in no time this too would pass.

In the meantime, crews came and went. Mother and Verlene drove over to see our "once lovely house." I remembered Mother's exact words, "I believe a flood is worse than a fire."

"No," Verlene said, "In a fire you lose all of your treasured family pictures."

"I guess you're right," Mother softly responded.

Anyway, that soggy mess of our house did pass. After months of work we moved into old familiar surroundings with new polish on the décor we had once chosen. I concluded when the floods go down on one's watered-down premises, life returns to normal again and a person can then see the whole thing from God's perspective.

Certainly, I was thankful that I could communicate with Jesus Christ as I surmounted the bridge across the flood.

As a child, I thought all streams were deep—four feet was indeed deep to me, but not deep at all to a tall man. To us, our rivers of difficulty are hurtful and deep, but to God they are mere streams in His ordered chain of events.

Adults, as well as children, must step onto the bridge.

BRIDGING YEARS OF TROUBLE TO TRANQUILITY

What are the speed bumps?----topics for thought and discussion:

1. Working while still recovering from surgery or other illness
2. Keeping on. Putting one foot in front of the other
3. Waiting for the results of diagnostic tests
4. Living with an illness that is chronic—that won't go away
5. Dealing with the fear of illness that is acute
6. Losing the entire fortune when a power plant is moved in beside the property; having no hope

Also, consider these speed bumps:

7. The everydayness of work is grinding one down to powder.
8. When best-laid plans fail—the remodeled church burns to the ground.
9. The house is perfectly put together and a water pipe bursts flooding the interior.
10. The boss overlooks you to promote someone else.
11. Your teenagers are not turning out like you had hoped.

12. Consequences of other people's behaviors are spilling over onto you.
13. Nothing seems permanent—security is lost.
14. Dreams are deferred—delayed until the next generation.

Hope "that thing with feathers that rests on the soul," wrote poet Emily Dickinson.

The story of Elijah serves as a timely reference in speed bump times. God's voice is gentle, not in the wind and the fire.

Psalm 63—The mind plays games, especially at night.

Bridging Years
of Trouble to Tranquility

CHAPTER 19

IN THE YEAR AFTER COLUMBINE, I VISITED THE HOLY LAND

Retirement does give one time to look at what is happening in our world, not simply to read the news, but to analyze it from the position of years of work experience—as a teacher, I taught at Memphis State for two years at night and during the summers while teaching full-time in high school for eighteen years. I saw first hand the stress students are under. Later when I became an administrative aide in high school, I had to deal daily with discipline problems and students cutting classes. Later, as an elementary principal, I again was in a position to deal with grievances between cafeteria workers, custodial crews, and the teaching staff. Stress exists in all work and school environments.

For over fifteen years now I have served my community as a member on a local school board because of a strong bond to young people in an educational setting. News regarding children, schools, and the field of education still catches my attention.

On April 20, 1999, the world watched in stunned silence as CNN televised students running out of Columbine High School in Littleton, Colorado. The news informed us that at least eighteen students were hospitalized and eleven had died in this very fine school of near 1800 enrollment. Two fellow students had sprayed bullets into the library, cafeteria, hallways, and classrooms. While nationally this was the 8th school shooting in which fellow students had opened fire in the past two years, the Columbine High School shooting gained enough press coverage with its more devastating results that the people of this country were awakened to the danger of what were once regular school days.

One can only imagine how such an event touches a retired school principal. For thirty years my purpose had been to be a role model, to exalt God in my demeanor as I taught and guided students. God had placed this desire in my heart when I was fifteen years old. As a high school teacher I supervised students both in class and at events in Detroit and other far-reaching field events. I had seen them interact in many environments. Never could I have imagined that one would turn on another and start shooting.

Early on, I saw first hand, the role that early religious training brings to students' lives. How far have we drifted since in 1968 we removed prayer and Bible reading from our schools? No longer do young people hear such verses as Psalm 145:1 **"I will bless thy name forever and ever."**

For me, one of the most troubling aspects of this turn to student violence is the familiar phrase, "No reason for shooting is known at this time." Is it possible that the nation's classrooms reflect our times and that the evil one is playing in the minds of our young students? How many of these young people are drawn to a new master who requires they greet him with lofty salutations, one who requires blood to satisfy his requirements?

I wonder—do you think Jell-o would ever jell if we continued to stir it? Satanic forces continue to stir the spirits of our young and old alike. He desires to whip into a frenzy old hurts and jealousies.

Violence has become a sign of our times and has now reached the very young. Day after day our students see evidence of such things as road rage, which increased 51% in the early 1990s our newscasters announced. The evil forces are having a heyday with the unsuspecting.

One November day as we drove near Townsend, Tennessee, we stopped for lunch and our young waiter shared with us that he has eight areas of his body pierced. In our brief conversation, he also shared that his mother and father had not had time to rear him so they gave him to his grandmother, who did the best she could. This young man needed to share his wounded life so much he opened up to total strangers how he had "tried" everything in Florida and had moved to Tennessee to get his life together again. I had worked with students too long not to see in his eyes a cry for help. Alone with him for a few minutes, I asked him if I could pray for him during my prayer time each day.

"Please do."

I pray Isaiah 11:2 for all of us, **"And the Spirit of the Lord shall rest upon him, the spirit of wisdom and understanding, the spirit of counsel and might, the spirit of knowledge and the fear of the Lord."**

God is the teacher—I am the student. I need only to obey the Master Teacher.

At times our land appears to groan under the weight of sin. In Hosea 4: 2, 3 we read:

"By swearing and lying, and killing, and stealing, and committing adultery, they break out, and blood toucheth blood. Therefore shall the land mourn, and everyone that dwelleth therein shall languish, with the beasts of the field, and with the fowl of heaven; Yea, the fishes of the sea also shall be taken away."

In January 17, 1999, we got to see first hand what appeared to be the groaning of nature. On an unseasonably warm Memphis day at 76 degrees in January, we packed our car and headed out of town. With thunderstorms forecast for later in the day, we started our journey.

First we came to Collierville where we noticed the light gray clouds were hovering lower and changing to a deep charcoal gray. Lightning flashed behind us, but in only 30 minutes, lightning began to encircle us. Before an hour had passed, we were in the center of 360 degrees of lightning—north, south, east and west—the sky remained illuminated.

So fascinatingly had this drama unfolded, I wanted to view the lightning from the center of the storm, but of course, to remain unharmed. I remember praying, "Lord, place us in the center of this storm, but don't allow it to hurt us."

In all of my life, I have never viewed a duplicate of what we witnessed from our car that evening. Something strange was unfolding. The heavens declared it. Nature was on a rampage. Houses and men were no match for its fury. Thunder rolled as we drove on. With the prelude to what would normally be torrential rain, our car moved on with only a few drops of rain touching our windows that night.

The lovely sunshine we had enjoyed had not warned us of storms on the horizon. Later on the evening news we heard about the havoc and devastation in three states—Arkansas, Tennessee and Mississippi. In only a few days, ninety tornadoes were sighted and mass destruction and death reigned over the cities of Jackson, Bolivar, Salisbury, Little Rock and Corinth. It was like a fierce tiger roaring down and exploding house about house—a baby dead here, a mother and daughter there, a pharmacist here and a laborer there. Trees snapped like the small twigs of child's play. How quickly our circumstances can change. How quickly have they changed in Littleton, Colorado; in towns in the paths of tornadoes; and in many other man-made and natural disasters.

As I look back, perhaps, for Drexel and me, our closes brush with death came in Amsterdam, Holland, when the right engine of our plane caught on fire. Our pilot announced, "We have an emergency! We will dump all of our fuel into the sea and head back to the airport for an emergency landing. Everyone remain in your seat. Again, this is an emergency!" The incident occurred on April 18, 1986 and as we watched the fuel streaming from the tanks, Drexel and I prayed through the thirty-minute process. In God's grace, the soil of Holland soon welcomed us and we were safe.

It only takes a moment for our circumstances to change; likewise it only takes a moment for our lives to change from lost to saved.

"God forgive me of my sins and accept me as one of your children because I accept you as Savior of my life."

Prayer is the weapon that helps us deal with the changes we face.

I am reminded of a true story told by my pastor:

Soldiers in Vietnam were under heavy fire. One soldier was seriously wounded, lying on the ground, begging as he yelled, "I'm hit. Please come back for me."

With bullets whizzing around his head, a sergeant set out to recover the wounded soldier, but withdrew. Another soldier looked down at the time on his watch. Soon he crawled out of the underbrush and proceeded through heavy fire to his fallen buddy who by now lay in a pool of blood. With bullets passing over their heads, he pulled his comrade to safety.

Later his commander asked him how he got the courage to place his life in such grave danger. He told his superior he had been watching the time on his watch and when the hands reached the exact time when his mother, back home, said she would be praying for him each day, he proceeded. He thought he had the best chance of making it to safety if he stepped out while she prayed for him.

He had faith in Mother's prayers-- Faith—a powerful weapon. A little faith removes great obstacles. More time to pray—the force and power of prayer is greater than any human force. God tells us there is security as we choose to walk with him.

> **"When thou passeth through the waters, I will be with thee, and through the rivers, they shall not overflow thee; when thou walkest through the fire, thou shalt not be burned; neither shall the flame kindle upon thee." Isaiah 43:2**

In all of our changing circumstances we have a promise—**"The Lord shall guide thee continually, and satisfy thy soul. " Isaiah 58:11**

Still hurting with the change in my own circumstances with Mother gone onto heaven, I decided to fulfill her life dream of going to the Holy Land. Years ago fighting between the Israelis and Arabs had caused the cancellation of my mother's flight. Now, as her daughter, I was headed for the Holy Land with the drums of Armageddon, as described in my recent study of Revelation 16:16, beating in my ears.

This trip to Israel, on June 5, 2000, had a profound effect upon my life. The Sea of Galilee, Jericho, the Dead Sea Scrolls, the Wailing Wall, the Dome of the Rock, Golgotha, and the Garden of Gethsemane—we saw all of these places.

On the final day of our trip, an event occurred that greatly affected my attitude. I stood with my first cousin Faye (Maude's daughter) at Megiddo, one of Solomon's chariot cities, and viewed the topography of the valley where the final battle of Armageddon would take place. As the Holy Spirit whispered to me, the words of a song flashed through my mind, "It is finished, the battle is over…it is finished, there'll be no more war…Jesus is Lord."

This, in itself, was touching, but a greater revelation was ahead as we left the Mount of Olives, drove into the Kidron Valley, and visited the Pool of Siloam and Hezekiah's Tunnel. Previously our guide informed us that the only remaining stone that was a part of Solomon's temple was the foundation stone of the Western Wall. That day he pointed out an area where David's palace had been located, the area where Solomon's palace stood, and the valley where the wives of Solomon lived.

My ears always perk up at the mention of Solomon, our name on Mother's side of the family. As I listened intently to his voice, I also heard the great voice of my Master revealing these words to me, "I have brought you back to your roots."

I was among family! My great grandfather John Moses Solomon had married a young maiden with red hair and blue eyes, Margaret Jane Young. Her relatives were from Ireland. So who was in Israel? Somehow I sensed that my mother's spirit was with me in Jerusalem and that her goal of going to the Holy Land had been fulfilled.

Also, on this final day of our trip, having already visited the house of the high priest Caiaphas, I stepped from our bus and lined up to thank our tour guide. He had shared with the group that he spoke five languages. As I thanked him, I also decided to ask him what "Eloi. Eloi, lama" means, for I had prayed this for H.C. and had never met anyone who knew Hebrew.

You were praying what Jesus prayed in the garden. You were praying, "My God, my God, why?" Here I was receiving the interpretation to a prayer I had prayed twenty-four years earlier.

Before I left Memphis, I purchased a new lock for my luggage. The young sales clerk volunteered to key my new lock for my piece of luggage for me. Since I had studied the book of Revelation so many times, the numbers 666 flashed to mind so I gave her my number. No! Momentarily panicky, I thought, my luggage will be lost with this Mark of the Beast on it. But then I reasoned that if God had given me these numbers just before she selected them, He would take care of my luggage.

"Key them---666," I told the clerk.

At the end of our tour in June, I learned the significance of this key number when our tour guide wrote his address, handed it to me: P. O. Box 666, and asked me to remember his family in prayer. A part of the puzzle had been revealed. What a confirmation!

Questions to Consider:

1. Do you have a portion of the Bible that you consider to be your specialty? If you did have one, which portion might it be?

2. Have you discovered the answer to a long held question years after you asked it?

3. Have you made an appointment at random, six months before you needed it and when the time came, realized that God had put the appointment on the exact day you needed it?

4. Knowing our circumstances can change in an instant, what do you do to prepare for such?

CHAPTER 20

Dreams and Their Relationship to the Bridge

Daniel 2:3 "And the king said unto them, I have dreamed a dream, and my spirit was troubled to know the dream."

Daniel 2:19 "Then was the secret revealed unto Daniel in a night vision. Then Daniel blessed the God of heaven."

Just as God had indeed used a dream for his purposes when He wanted me to tell Hobert, Elease, and Hobert, Jr. the contents of that dream, He has visited me in seven different dreams in my lifetime. I have always told God, "If my will is too stubborn for you to use during the daytime, use me at night while I sleep."

The insight God has given me through these dreams of revelation has carried me to deeper heights of spiritual growth. Certainly there is a difference in a child's nightmare and a dream brought on by having eaten a heavy meal before bedtime and one that contains the unmistakable voice of God. I have learned to discern which is which.

God's power is awesome and inexplicable. My brain cannot think on his level. I believe God can use my stubborn will more effectively when I am asleep.

Also, I have found that the more I study my Bible and pray, the more usable I am.

I compare the Old and New Testament passages concerning dreams:

Joel 2:28 "And it shall come to pass afterward, that I will pour out my spirit upon all flesh…your old men shall dream dreams, your young men shall see visions."

Acts 2:17 "And it shall come to pass in the last days, saith God, I will pour out of my spirit upon all flesh…, and your young men shall see visions, and your old men shall dream dreams."

On November 24, 1996, an article appeared in the Ft. Myers, Florida, News-Press under the headline, "Success Born of Tragedy." The writer depicted a dream, which led an author to write the novel, *Deep End of the Ocean*. The author, Jacquelyn Mitchard of Madison, Wisconsin, told how tragedy struck her life in 1993 when her husband Dan Allegretti was diagnosed with colon cancer and died a few months later.

She was given inspiration to write by her husband's advice just before he slipped into coma. "You're going to be so far from here; just believe in yourself."

In the article, Mitchard stated she did not believe in signs or prophecies, but she did think there was such a phenomena as believing in someone so much that you give them confidence.

While we differ here, since I believe in the prophecies of the Bible, still I connected with some of what the author had to say on the subject of dreams.

Mitchard said she was inordinately impressed by the narrative quality of this dream she had, a dream that came to her complete in its storyline. Immediately, she wrote it down on some paper beside her bed...and that was the end of that experience. Or so she thought.

"Nothing like that had ever happened to me before, and when I say it, it sounds like I've thrown a rod or something like that. Because I'm not a gazer into crystals. I'm just an ordinary, once-born kind of person."

Jacqueline Mitchard possessed less than $100 when she quit her job to write this novel using the storyline of that dream. Soon after it was published, it rose to #1 on the New York Times Bestseller List.

As I read about Mitchard's experience with a dream, I was prompted to recall my own dreams—seven dreams that had influenced my life in some specific way, just as hers had influenced her to write this novel.

I have already shared the first two dreams—dreams that had a profound effect on me.

Dream #3 1980:

I view three teenagers that I had never seen—one boy and two girls, each with dark brown eyes and hair. In my dream they belong in my family line.

I hear my own voice speak as I place my hand on the shoulder of the young man.

I say, "Be thou blessed of God."

Next, I move to the older girl with the long brown curls falling down over her shoulders. I repeat the same blessing:

"Be thou blessed of God."

Next, I move to the attractive youngest teenager, and placing my hand upon her shoulder, I repeat:

"Be thou <u>very</u> blessed of God."

Then I feel myself draw back with the thought: You are being partial to the baby girl.

God's words immediately clarified that admonition: "No, you did not bless them. I did. I will bless whom I choose."

Later that year I revised my will to include these three individuals. Peace came over me, and from that day, faith for future generations grew in my heart. Although the fulfillment may not come to pass in my lifetime, I feel certain it will come to pass.

By faith Abraham! Hebrews 11: 13 flashed to mind.

Dream #4------September 1984

Before this dream I had memorized Daniel 2: 20-22, a passage which begins with a blessing to God:

Daniel answered and said, **"Blessed be the name of God forever and ever: for wisdom and might are his: and he changeth the times and the seasons: he removeth kings and sitteth up kings: he giveth wisdom unto the wise, and knowledge to them that know understanding: he revealeth the deep and secret things: he knoweth what is in the darkness, and the light dwelleth with him."**

On one occasion I have even shared this passage with an area school superintendent whose sibling was near death. We had joined in prayer for his relative.

During August-September 1984, I prayed asking God to reveal to me some of the deep and secret things mentioned in Daniel 2:22. I told him I desired to have a more intimate relationship with him, and that I longed to bring him glory. Also, I had read in the book of Daniel that God had given this young lad the interpretation of King Nebuchadnezzer's dream in order for the king to know **"the most high…in the kingdom of men and**

giveth to whomever he will" (Daniel 4:25). I, too, wanted to know more about how God ruled on earth as well as in heaven.

One evening in September, the Lord spoke to my heart through a dream: If you will give up reading novels, I shall reveal to you deep and secret things.

Being an avid reader, I was shaken for the message struck a familiar chord. As I looked over my lifetime of reading, I saw a very tall stack of novels. At age 14, I had read *Jane Eyre* and *Wuthering Heights*, plus almost every well-known book in my hometown library. In fact, I had made a deliberate tally of my reading in the first six months of 1994---20 novels! This tally represented a lifelong habit I had proudly cultivated.

Besides, relaxation comes from reading. Everyone needs to relax. Reading helped me to unwind at night. Therefore, for me to give up the reading of novels was truly "a sacrifice of praise."

In fact, I recall communicating with God about it:

Do you know what you are asking of me?

Mulling the matter in my mind, I asked myself, Will the sacrifice be worth the promise?

Finally, I replied, Lord, I do not want to make a promise I cannot keep. I promise to give up reading novels for the next three months. I know I can do that. Then we will just go from there. For now, I must make a promise I can keep.

Those three months stretched to five–to six months, and I started channeling my time to reading chapters in the Bible and to praying for more people. Now it has become a routine every morning and every night. I am a better person because of this procedure.

Dream #5----December 8, 1994

I had a dream of warning. In the dream my husband Drexel had become uncharacteristically frightened. Being a cautious man, a circumspect individual, Drexel was never one to place his life in danger, yet in this dream he did so. Without hesitation, he had jumped into shallow water, but the quicksand, which was invisible to the eye, had pulled him under. Minutes passed. He was not coming up. Fearing for his life, I heard myself pray, "Lord, spare his life in the Name of Jesus."

Two days after this troubling dream, we were scheduled to fly to Florida. At 5:00 a.m. on this dark, rainy morning, Drexel was loading our luggage and camcorder into the car. Suddenly, he heard something, but in the dark, saw nothing.

As he went around to the other side of the car, a man, a stranger, appeared. My husband said, "Stand where you are—don't come any closer."

Totally ignoring this admonition, the young man continued in his approach. His excuse---he was looking for his cat. When he did not stop, Drexel warned, "Stop or we will call the police." When this command did not deter the man, Drexel yelled to me to call the police.

Oddly, the evening before, I had reviewed the emergency phone numbers posted by my kitchen telephone. For no apparent reason, I had memorized the phone number for the Germantown Police Department.

I dialed.

The man vanished before the police arrived.

Assuming the episode was handled, I went to my side of the car to finish packing. As I placed my carry-on bag inside, I noticed the camcorder had been removed from the backseat and was sitting in the grass in the rain. The man had left in a hurry without stealing the object he had wanted.

As we drove to the airport, we concluded the man had seen Drexel loading luggage and he was approaching to rob him.

Thankfully, I had prayed for my husband after I had seen the frightful scene in the dream. God's constant care of us comforts us and gives us peace of mind. I recalled that in the dream I had blurted out, "God, spare his life in the Name of Jesus.

It pays to pray ahead.

Dream # 6-----July 6, 1991

Asleep in the Rich Building in downtown Savannah, Tennessee, after driving to my hometown for an appointment, I dreamed I was standing at the top of the stairway on the second floor of the building. Since this building has two stairways, I specifically noted I was on the back section of the stairs where Dr. Murle Sinquefield's dental office and Dr. E. Alton Akes' optometry office used to be when I was a child. As I viewed the three sections of this stairway, I was amazed that the wool runner on the stairway was made from the most beautiful Persian print with vibrant, sharp red and blue colors.

In this dream, I viewed the Persian runner (with the knowledge that it had been purchased by a young attorney) covering the three sections of stairs.

At the basement level of the building there was an open room with chairs and benches occupied by people who were either praying silently or moving freely giving encouragement to those praying with a touch or a hug. A sense of peace permeated the room—a sense of unity prevailed.

I was captivated by the presence of a woman who almost glided from one individual to another, placing her arms around each. The love of God radiated from her. Individuals who entered the room, left with peace, comfort and an assurance that God would carry them through whatever they might encounter.

On the east side of this room was an altar. God was individually answering each prayer.

Joy abounded.

Faith flourished.

Over ten years have passed since I dreamed this dream. Why had the rugs been so important to me? Why had God placed an attorney in my dream? What was the connection to the sanctuary of peace?

Today I do not have all the answers. But I am confident that some day I will know. Since my living room in the apartment of the Rich building had often been a place of prayer, the dream inspired me to praise and to never overlook the need to pray.

The answer to the question—Why had God placed an attorney in my dream?—was answered on my birthday, October 29, 1999, when we sold the Rich building to a young Savannah attorney. The old land deeds revealed this same lot was the former location of the law office of Ross and Ross.

Dream #7 The Dream of Calling

Scott , a young man in my church, attended a Christian high school and upon graduation enrolled in a Christian college to train for some type of Christian work as a lay person, minister or missionary.

With his straw blonde hair, Scott was extremely good looking with twinkling blue eyes that did not cover up his fun-loving nature. In fact, his sense of humor and boyish pranks sometimes got him into trouble.

Possibly it was then that I, as an educator, took a special interest in Scott. It was at this time I had a dream about him:

I saw Scott and his earthly father arm wrestling in the church office. A great love for his son emanated from the father's heart. Simultaneously, as they wrestled, I heard a booming voice from above, "I have called you. Yea, I have called you."

Wondering what it meant, I kept the dream to myself.

One month later, after church services, I was nudged by the Holy Spirit to share this dream with his father. Not wanting to do this, I reluctantly told Scott's father.

Weeks later Scott came to the church office and the two of them prayed. Scott's father then shared this dream. Scott reacted by saying:

"I have always known I was called to preach. The calling has been on my heart since I was a child."

Years passed.

Today, Scott, his wife Laura and their three children are missionaries in India, and I am reminded of the dream about him. A call from God has placed Scott in India where as a missionary, he, a Christian in the minority, finds that Hinduism is the dominate religion. When Scott came home on leave, I asked his permission to share this dream.

Today, the dreams are as vivid as they were years ago, but I do not understand exactly how God works. All I know is if God works in this way, who am I to command that he does not have power and authority in dreams? I desire to be a willing recipient for messages from the Master if they bring glory to Him.

> **Jeremiah 33:3 "Call unto me, and I will answer thee, and shew thee great and mighty things which thou knowest not."**

Why do feelings of surprise and delight surge through me as I think about dreams in the Bible and their relationship to the Bridge? His constant care of us continues to make me stand in awe. The waters may rage beneath me as I cross troubled waters in my life, but I know that this Bridge is no drawbridge nor is it a swinging rope bridge. I do not have to fear the turbulent, murky waters in the canyons of my stressful day-to-day schedule, because the Bridge is never moving, always present, strong and sturdy—"omnipotent." Revelation 19:6

Questions to Consider:

1. Has God ever spoken to you through a dream?

2. How are such messages from God different from those of the occult?

3. Since we know God often warns of impending danger, how do you plan to draw closer to Him so he can communicate warnings to you?

Building A Relationship
Based Upon Faith

THE BRIDGE

The Bible states that God gives us the desires of our hearts if we meet the conditions written in the Word of God, and as I reflected on my greatest desire as a child of twelve, as an adult of thirty, or as an individual of fifty, it was the same desire—that all of my family would be saved and would spend eternity with God.

My life is the story of an educator who led children through some of the most horrendous times in history—the explosion of the Challenger, JFK's assassination, and the murder of Dr. Martin Luther King, but these were not the main threads of my life. The fact that I was an educator was incidental to my real goal. I was a Christian who just happened to work for thirty years in the field of education, but my main goal in life was to live a life that would give glory to God and to make sure that everyone in my circle of friends and family prepared themselves for their heavenly reward.

This is a chronicle of exactly how God worked to achieve His will through this educator–a prayer that was breathed to the throne of God in 1947 was not answered until 1974; another facet of that prayer was brought to fruition in 1999. The span of years and the time frame did not matter—what did matter was that everyone who passed on to eternity met Jesus face to face because of this right decision.

Different individuals in this book made their unique preparation to face God in ways that coincided with their personality; some went into their last hours almost holding back on the reigns, but ultimately they made the RIGHT decision.

WHICH CHOICE WILL YOU MAKE?

WILL YOU CHOOSE TO TAKE THE BRIDGE, OR WILL YOU CONTINUE TO SWIM AGAINST THE CURRENT?

It is not a coincidence that you are reading this book. It was all in God's plan for you, and today, if you do not have this Bridge—

do not have this personal relationship with your Creator, I trust that the prompting of the Holy Spirit will draw you to Him as it did me when I was a child of eleven years old.

You ask, "How can I do this? I am not good enough. How do I make my first step toward the Bridge? How can I be assured of eternal life when I die?"

In our world, after the events of 9-11—after the twin towers in New York were brought to the ground by two airplanes, after the threat of germ and nuclear warfare from Iraq and the possiblity of more terrorism in the United States, and after the spread of the West Nile virus, we have a potential, world-wide epidemic of SARS in 2003.

I saw the West Nile virus rear its ugly head in my courtyard and kill a beautiful blue jay. Only the day before, this bird had sprinkled the air with its flute-like notes and its thrills of clear, sharp melody. Today, it lay dead three feet from my sunroom windows. If one mosquito with 47 teeth can take the life of a much larger bird—then I have to be on guard against little things—one stolen scarf from a department, one bar of candy taken by a child, or one ream of paper taken from the company that we work for—this will not matter we erroneously make ourselves believe.

Little sins do spread, and if you are not sure how you stand with God, now is the time. You are making a decision by doing nothing. you are saying NO.

Read the invitation which follows and mean it with your heart—then you will be transformed into His image by His righteousness—not your own goodness, because you cannot be good enough within yourself. Nobody can. God knew that we could never be strong and be good enough, so He has taken care of that aspect for us—His children.

Last week at the age of 98, my favorite elementary teacher, Mrs. D. G. White, went to be with her Creator. Her gentle spirit calmed my seven-year-old fears in the third grade; even a young child has worries and problems. Adults have no monopoly on fear.

Where will you spend eternity?

"But those who still reject me are like the restless sea . . . . There is no peace, says my God, for them!" Isaiah 57:20-21 TLB

Invitation to Stop Fording the Stream When a Bridge Has Been Provided

PLEASE REPEAT ALOUD THESE WORDS INVITING CHRIST INTO YOUR HEART:

Dear God,

Could it be that you would call me your own? That you would want to recognize my sin no more? I have done many things that do not live up to your will for my life. I confess all of these wrongs and ask for your forgiveness. I believe that Jesus died for my sins, and that His grace is for me too. I want that in my life. Thank you, God, for saving me for all eternity. Amen.

Now you are on the road to being ALIVE IN CHRIST!

God Bless *You*.

"Let justice roll on like a river, righteousness like a never-failing stream." Amos 5: 24 NIV

The End

JUST FOR YOUR INFORMATION:

Betty worked in the field of education for thirty years as a teacher and elementary school principal. She has also taught Sunday school, Bible studies, and seminars. She is listed in the following books: 2000 Notable American Women; Outstanding Leaders in Elementary & Secondary Education; Who's Who in American Education; The World Who's Who of Women; et al.

ENDORSEMENTS

From time to time, we all can benefit from those whom God sent before us to build a bridge–a safe passage over sometimes dangerous waters. The Bridge will reinforce that when faced with a perilous journey, the bridge needed may already be in place.

Barry Hendon, DVM

I have been acquainted with Betty Hendon for almost fifty years and am very pleased to endorse her book–The Bridge. She has always been a fine Christian woman, wife, mother, teacher and certainly a friend. Her love of God and faith in God are evident in every aspect of her life. This is clearly demonstrated in her autobiographic book–The Bridge.

Dr. Virgil H. Crowder

I stood beside Betty Hendon as we "crossed the bridge" of turbulent times in education and witnessed first hand the faith she had in the Lord Jesus Christ. This book would make excellent reading for both the "new" Christian and one who has long been journeying along the road of Christian Faith. Take a leap of faith with her as she tells her story.

Jan Thomson, Librarian & Bible Teacher